D1472581

The Manager and His Values:
An International Perspective

The Manager and His Values:

An International Perspective
from The United States,
Japan, Korea, India,
and Australia

George W. England

Professor of Psychology and Industrial Relations
University of Minnesota

Ballinger Publishing Company • Cambridge, Mass.
A Subsidiary of J.B. Lippincott Company

This book is printed on recycled paper.

Copyright © 1975 by Ballinger Publishing Company. All rights reserved. No part of this publication may be reproduced, stored in a retrieval system, or transmitted in any form or by any means, electronic mechanical photo-copy, recording or otherwise, without the prior written consent of the publisher.

International Standard Book Number: 0-88410-288-2

Library of Congress Catalog Card Number: 75-31833

Printed in the United States of America

Library of Congress Cataloging in Publication Data

England, George W.
  The manager and his values.

  Bibliography: p.
  1. Executives—Case studies. 2. Social values. 3. Worth. I. Title.
HF5500.2.E54   658.4   75-31833
ISBN 0-88410-288-2

HF
5500.2
.E54

Contents

162422

List of Tables

List of Figures

Preface

This book is the culmination of nearly ten years of study and research concerning the personal value systems of managers in the United States, Japan, Korea, India and Australia. The author is indebted to many institutions and to many individuals who assisted in this effort to better understand managers, their value systems and their behavior. Professors Arthur M. Whitehill, Jr. (University of Hawaii) and Shin-ichi Takezawa (Rikkyo University, Tokyo) are largely responsible for introducing me to both the complexity and the possibilities inherent in cross-national comparative research. Their interest and cooperation as well as the model provided by their own significant study, *The Other Worker*, have been of great value to my efforts. Professors Thomas A. Mahoney, Herbert G. Heneman, Jr., Marvin D. Dunnette and Robert T. Holt, colleagues at the University of Minnesota, have been unfailing in providing enthusiastic support and scholarly evaluation as this research has progressed from year to year. Colleagues such as these are constantly sought but seldom found.

Financial assistance and research cooperation have come from a variety of institutions including the Industrial Relations Center, University of Minnesota; Graduate School of Business Administration, University of Minnesota; Center for Comparative Study of Technological and Social Change, University of Minnesota; Midwestern Universities Consortium for International Activities; Ford Foundation; American Philosophical Society; Office of Naval Research; Shri Ram Centre for Industrial Relations, New Delhi, India; Australian Institute of Management; Department of Economics, University of Western Australia; and Institute of Technology and Development, East-West Center, Honolulu, Hawaii. The generous support of these institutions is gratefully acknowledged.

During the course of these studies, many individuals at other institutions and in other countries have provided valuable help. Those who have made major contributions are Mr. Blair Denniston, director, Australian Institute of Management; Mr. O.P. Dhingra, assistant director, Shri Ram Centre for Industrial Relations; Professor Pjtor Hesseling, University of Rotterdam; Professor K.D. Kim, North Carolina State University; Mr. Ryohji Koike, Nippon Kokan K.K. Co., Tokyo; Dr. T. Roger Manley, Wright-Patterson Air Force Base; Professor Anant Negandhi, Kent State University; and Professor Desmond Oxnam, University of Western Australia.

Many former students have worked as colleagues in this research effort and have made important contributions of all types. Professor Naresh C. Agarwal, McMasters University, Hamilton, Ontario, Canada; and Mr. Raymond Lee, Hennepin County Personnel Department, have been closely associated with the research for the past four years and have aided me in more ways than I can recount. Richard E. Henderson, Dr. Timothy J. Keaveny, Karen A. Olsen, Nancy Rydel Dewitt, Robert E. Trerise, Professor Myron L. Weber and William T. Whitely will all recognize their contributions in this volume.

Marjorie Whitehill and Donna D'Andrea of the University of Minnesota Industrial Relations Center have provided first-rate secretarial skills for nearly ten years on this and related publications. I am deeply appreciative for all they have done.

My wife Bea and our four children, Paula, Mark, Brad and Julie, have provided a family atmosphere that could withstand the rigors of research, travel and writing schedules. It is with deep gratitude and love that this book is dedicated to Bea England, the finest human being I know.

George W. England
Industrial Relations Center
University of Minnesota
August 1975

Chapter One

The Nature of our Inquiry

This book presents a study of the personal value systems of over 2500 managers in five countries: the United States of America, Japan, Korea, India and Australia. The ideas and data presented stem from a long-term research project aimed at the description, measurement and understanding of the personal value systems of managers and the impact of values on behavior. A personal value system is viewed as a relatively permanent perceptual framework which shapes and influences the general nature of an individual's behavior. Values are similar to attitudes but are more ingrained, permanent and stable in nature. Likewise, a value is seen as being more general and less tied to any specific referent object than is the case with many attitudes. Value, as used here, is closer to ideology or philosophy than it is to attitude.

Managers of business organizations, vitally important in any industrial or industrializing society, represent individuals whose values are of particular interest. The significance and importance of studying the value systems of managers is seen when one considers seriously the following reasonable assertions and their implications:

1. Personal value systems influence the way a manager looks at other individuals and groups of individuals, thus influencing interpersonal relationships.
2. Personal value systems influence a manager's perceptions of situations and problems he faces.
3. Personal value systems influence a manager's decisions and solutions to problems.
4. Personal value systems influence the extent to which a manager will accept or will resist organizational pressures and goals.
5. Personal value systems influence not only the perceptions of individual and organizational success, but their achievement as well.
6. Personal value systems set the limits for the determination of what is and what is not ethical behavior by a manager.

1

7. Personal value systems provide a meaningful level of analysis for comparative studies among national and organizational groupings of individuals.

RATIONALE FOR THE STUDY

A framework was developed to delineate the relationship of values to behavior for managers and was subsequently utilized in the development of a measurement approach to personal value systems that (1) was responsive to relevant theoretical and definitional notions of contemporary value theory, (2) was designed in light of the characteristics of the group being studied (managers) and (3) was clearly cognizant of the primary importance of the behavioral relevance and significance of values.

Several major classes of overlapping values are recognized in the framework as shown in Figure 1-1. All possible values which might be held by an individual or by a specific group constitute the total value space and are known as *potential values*. The potential values are made up of two classes of values: *nonrelevant* or *weak values* for a specific group of individual (those which would have little or no impact on behavior) and *conceived values* (those which may be translated from the intentional state into behavior). Conceived values are made up of *operative values* (those which have a relatively high probability of being translated from the intentional state into actual behavior), *intended values* (those which are viewed as important but may have only a moderate probability of being translated from the intentional state into behavior because of situational factors) and *adopted values* (those which are less a part of the personality structure of the individual and affect behavior largely because of situational factors).

The development of the Personal Values Questionnaire (PVQ) was based on the rationale that the meanings attached by an individual to a carefully specified set of concepts will provide a useful description of his personal value system, which may in turn be related to his behavior in systematic ways. This

Figure 1-1. Value Framework

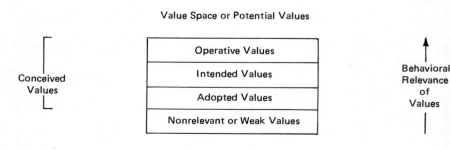

Value Space or Potential Values

Conceived Values

| Operative Values |
| Intended Values |
| Adopted Values |
| Nonrelevant or Weak Values |

Behavioral Relevance of Values

attempt to describe an individual's values through the use of a carefully specified set of concepts was influenced by the work of Charles Osgood (1957) and his associates and represents an adaptation of their methodology.

In order to specify a set of concepts relevant to the personal value systems of managers, a pool of 200 concepts was selected from literature dealing with organizations and with individual and group behavior. In addition, ideological and philosophical concepts were included to represent major belief systems. A panel of expert judges reduced this pool to a set of 96 concepts, which was further reduced to 66 concepts based on pilot studies. To provide a framework within which respondents could conveniently evaluate each concept, the concepts were divided into five categories: goals of business organizations, personal goals of individuals, groups of people and institutions, ideas associated with people, and ideas about general topics.

In the PVQ for managers, four scales are used to represent two modes of valuation. Since the general value of an object or idea to an individual is thought to be largely a function of its degree of importance to him, the primary or power mode of valuation utilized is the importance scale, which consists of three points—high, average and low. Because of the emphasis on the behavioral effect of values, it was deemed necessary to make operational the theoretical distinction between the intentionality of values and their translation into behavior. To the extent that it is possible to determine a consistent rationale as to why an individual or a specific group thinks certain concepts are important, one has a reasonable basis for determining the behavioral significance of different classes of values. In this process, three secondary modes of valuation were developed from the literature.

The *pragmatic* mode of valuation suggests that an individual has an evaluative framework that is primarily guided by success-failure considerations: will a certain course of action work or not; how successful or unsuccessful is it apt to be. The pragmatic mode of valuation runs throughout much of the literature dealing with managers and finds support in various analyses of the Allport-Vernon-Lindzey *Study of Values* which suggest a major dimension of values as being "pragmatic and utilitarian" or the finding of a major value factor being "idealism vs. practicality."

The *ethical-moral* mode of valuation implies an evaluative framework consisting of ethical considerations influencing behavior toward actions and decisions which are judged to be "right" and away from those judged to be "wrong." The existence of a moral-ethical orientation is at the very heart of most religious beliefs and is supported by analyses of the *Study of Values* which find value dimensions or factors such as "social and altruistic" and "idealism."

The *affect of feeling* mode of valuation suggests an evaluative framework which is guided by hedonism; one behaves in ways that increase pleasure and decrease pain. The affective component of values has an extensive philosophical and psychological background and seemed important to include as an orientation in the present study.

In the PVQ, the pragmatic mode of valuation is represented by a "successful" scale; the ethical-moral mode of valuation is obtained through a "right" scale; and the affect or feeling mode of valuation is measured through use of a "pleasant" scale.

A combination of primary and secondary modes of valuation was thought to be a better behavioral predictor than would be either mode alone. For example, if Manager A is generally pragmatically oriented (i.e., concepts which were important to him were also seen as being successful as opposed to right or pleasant), his behavior would be predicted best by viewing it as a joint function of those concepts he thought were *important* and *successful.* In a more general sense, what is being suggested is that an individual's behavior (insofar as it is influenced by his personal values) is best explained by utilizing both those things he considers important and his personal primary orientation. Symbolically, one could say:

$$B_v \longrightarrow f(I \cap PO)_c$$

This expression would be read: the behavior of an individual, insofar as behavior is a function of values, is best indicated by the joint function of those concepts he considers important and which fit his primary orientation. For a pragmatically oriented individual, behavior is best indicated by those concepts considered important and successful; for a morally-ethically oriented individual, behavior is best predicted by those concepts considered important and right; while for an affect-oriented individual, behavior is best predicted by those concepts considered important and pleasant.

This, then, is the general rationale for the study reported. Our starting point is the individual manager in a work organization; our interest is in his personal values and what they tell us about his work behavior and outcomes of this behavior. We are not studying organizations, industries, nations or cultures although each manager in our studies certainly can be placed within these broader frames of reference. It is apparent, however, that we must aggregate the individual results to focus on many questions of interest.

SUMMARY OF STUDY RESULTS

While detailed results will be presented in the chapters that follow, it seems appropriate to indicate the general nature of our findings at the outset.

1. There are large individual differences in personal values within each group we have studied. Among managers in each country, some have a pragmatic orientation (they view ideas and concepts in terms of whether or not they work or are successful), some have an ethical-moral orientation (they view ideas in terms of being right or wrong), while a few have an affect or feeling orientation (they view ideas in terms of whether or not they are pleasant). Some

managers have a very small set of values while others have a large set and seem to be influenced by many strongly held values. The important values of some managers include concepts which are almost solely related to their organizational life while other managers include a wide range of personal and philosophical concepts among their important values. Some managers have what might be termed individualistic values as opposed to group-oriented values. Some managers are highly achievement-oriented as opposed to others who value status and prestige more highly. Finally, it is clear that some managers have a personal value system that might be characterized as "hard." Their important values include concepts such as Ambition, Obedience, Aggressiveness, Achievement, Success, Competition, Risk and Force. Other managers have value systems that are often characterized as "soft" and include such concepts as Loyalty, Trust, Cooperation, Compassion, Tolerance, Employee Welfare, Social Welfare and Religion. Personal value systems, then, are like most other human characteristics; individuals differ greatly with respect to them.

2. Personal value systems of managers are relatively stable and do not change rapidly. In 1966 we measured the personal value systems of a national sample of U.S. managers. In 1972, Professors Edward Lusk and Bruce Oliver of the University of Pennsylvania Wharton School repeated our earlier study on a comparable national sample of U.S. managers. They reasoned that the widespread airing of environmental and social issues (e.g., pollution, the Vietnam war, lifestyle changes, changing expectation of the labor force, and minority and disadvantaged group employment problems) between 1966 and 1972 would be accompanied by changes in the value systems of managers. However, the differences between the value systems of the 1966 sample and the 1972 sample of managers were very small. Over all 66 concepts in the PVQ, the average difference in value importance was only 3.3 percentage points between the two time periods. A difference of 10 percent or greater between the two samples was found on only four of the 66 concepts. (The 1972 sample placed greater value on the concepts Dignity, Trust and Change, and lower value on the concept My Boss as compared to the 1966 sample.) These results show quite clearly that the personal value systems of 1972 managers are very similar to those of 1966 managers, and thus would not appear to change rapidly even during periods of environmental and social flux. A probable explanation of this stability would involve the nature of the selection and developmental process managers go through, the requirements and constraints that the job of managing places upon managers, and the fact that personal values are a relatively stable human characteristic.

3. Personal value systems of managers are related to and/or influence the way managers behave on the job. While several of our analyses show this to be the case, the clearest evidence emerges in the study of Indian and Australian managers. Here we assessed the personal values of each manager and measured his behavior on five job incidents, each representing a typical problem

which a manager might encounter in the performance of his job. Prior to analyzing the data, we made 25 predictions about how managers with certain values would be expected to behave. Examples of these predictions are: (a) managers who have profit maximization as an important goal will be less willing to spend money on cafeteria and rest room facility improvements than will managers who do not have profit maximization as an important value; (b) managers for whom compassion is an important value would be less willing to obtain research and development funds by depriving employees of part of a potential wage increase than would managers for whom compassion is not an important value; and (c) managers for whom cooperation is an important value would promote individual B to be their assistant more than would managers for whom cooperation is not an important value given the following choices:

> Individual A is a very creative man who has been constantly making suggestions for improvement in office procedures. Although all his ideas are not practical ones, you have in the past adopted some of his suggestions. A is sincere and hard working, and he can be very helpful to others if he is asked for his help. He is, however, not a very popular man in the department, because other employees do not like procedural changes and extra pressures which they think are unnecessary at times.

> Individual B, equally efficient as A, is not a man of ideas. He, on the other hand, is a very congenial and well-liked person. He goes out of the way to help others whenever they have problems and is definitely contributing to the good morale of your department. He enjoys the reputation of a kind man.

Across all five indicents, 19 out of 25 predictions are supported by the data for Indian managers and 18 of 25 predictions are supported for Australian managers. These results offer strong support for the contention that values are related to behavior in meaningful ways for managers. The fact that the relationships exist within samples of managers from many different organizations all across India and Australia and from managers with varied organizational and personal backgrounds is clear evidence of the role of personal values in influencing problem-solving and decision-making behavior. Personal values are certainly important in understanding and predicting the behavior of managers.

4. Personal value systems of managers are related to their career success as managers. We defined career success or personal success in terms of managerial pay relative to the manager's age in our study of American, Japanese, Indian and Australian managers. It was our judgment that the heterogeneous nature of our samples dictated that we measure success in terms of objective data that were relatively easy to collect. Relative salary level for one's age group

provided such a measure which was sufficiently accurate for our purposes. We then developed and cross-validated a value profile key or pattern that was related to success in each of the four countries. The value patterns that were related to success were similar in the four countries and correlated with success as follows: U.S.A. (.32), Australia (.47), India (.35) and Japan (.26). These correlations are of similar magnitude to the validity coefficients generally reported for predicting manager success by other types of predictors. We view these results as solid evidence that value patterns and success are meaningfully related in a similar fashion across the four countries.

Viewing the value-success relationships for managers in the four countries provides the following picture. Successful managers favor pragmatic, dynamic, achievement-oriented values while less successful managers prefer more static and passive values, the latter forming a framework descriptive of organizational stasis rather than organizational and environmental flux. More successful managers favor an achievement orientation and prefer an active role in interaction with other individuals useful in achieving the managers' organizational goals. They value a dynamic environment and are willing to take risks to achieve organizationally valued goals. Relatively less successful managers have values associated with a static, protected environment in which they take relatively passive roles and often enjoy extended seniority in their organizational positions.

Since the value systems of American managers seem relatively stable over time and since values are related to success, we have explored the possibility of using values as a selection or promotion device in attempting to pick people who will turn out to be successful. Table 1-1 shows that value patterns are predictive of success and could be used in selection and placement decisions. We are hesitant, however, to recommend the use of personal values in selection because we do not know the full consequences of an individual organization having managers with similar value profiles. Persuasive arguments can be made that organizational vitality and adaptation to changing social and technological conditions may come about in large part because of the value mix in an organization. There may well be some optimum range of value differences within an organization; we simply do not know what that optimal range is for any given organization.

Table 1-1. Chances in 100 of Being Among the Top Half of Managers in Terms of Success

Value Score		*Success Expectancy*
Very High	(top 20 percent)	72
High	(next 20 percent)	63
Medium	(next 20 percent)	47
Low	(next 20 percent)	41
Very Low	(bottom 20 percent)	34

5. There are differences in personal values of managers working in *different organizational contexts*. One example of the impact of type of organization upon values is shown when we compare the personal values of American managers with those of American labor leaders.[1] In general, union leaders have a moralistic orientation while managers are pragmatic. Owners and Stockholders represent important values (likely to influence behavior) for managers and weak values (unlikely to influence behavior) for union leaders. Similarly, Blue Collar Workers and Laborers represent important values for union leaders and weak values for managers. As regards organizational goals, Employee Welfare and Social Welfare are important values for union leaders and weak values for managers. Just the opposite is true for High Productivity, Organizational Stability, Organizational Growth, Organizational Efficiency and Industry Leadership. Finally, Ambition, Ability and Skill represent important values for managers while Trust, Loyalty and Honor are much less important. For union leaders, just the reverse is found. These differences help explain why the two groups approach various issues from conflicting directions. Perhaps it is only the recognition of mutual dependence as a fundamental aspect of modern industrial relations that allows cooperation between the groups to result even though it may be, as some writers have suggested, "antagonistic" in nature.

An example where organizational setting does not make a difference is found when we compare Indian managers from the private sector with those from the public sector. Despite the basic differences in setting, there is great similarity between the value profiles of public and private sector managers.[2] The profiles of the two groups correlated 0.98 and are almost identical. Although this high degree of similarity is surprising, it may result in part because the private sector is a primary source of managerial talent for the public sector and because of the social pressure for public sector firms to view private sector companies as ideals in some respects so as to become viable economic units. These forces may result in public sector managers having values and concerns which are typical of private sector managers.

A final example of the impact of organizational variables upon value systems is found when we look at value differences between managers employed in firms of different size.[3] In an analysis of American, Japanese and Korean managers, we defined large firms as those with 5000 or more employees, medium size firms as those with 500-4999 employees and small firms as those with 1-499 employees. In all three countries, there was a general trend of organizational goals being a more important part of managers' value systems in large firms, less so in medium size firms and least important in small firms. This

---

[1] A study using the PVQ with union leaders forms the basis for this comparison. Detailed results are available in England, Agarwal and Trerise (1971).

[2] A sample of 263 managers in public companies (government owned) in India was studied in addition to the managers from private companies.

[3] For more detailed results, see England and Lee (1973).

was the case for the goals High Productivity, Profit Maximization, Organizational Growth, Organizational Efficiency and Industry Leadership. There was no relationship between size and the importance of the goals Organizational Stability and Social Welfare. The patterns in each of the three countries were similar and suggest to us that the effects of environmental uncertainty, organizational complexity and conflicting organizational goals in large organizations may explain these findings. One might logically assume that as organizations increase in size, managers are confronted with more difficult, more complex, more ambiguous and more challenging decisions. Communication and interpersonal relationships also become more complex and difficult, and goal clashes become inevitable. The consequences of these management and coordination problems undoubtedly are more challenging in large firms than in small firms and, therefore, influence top managers of large firms to be more aware of organizational goals and to ferret out deviations and to establish systems of controls and incentives which ensure internal conformity with the firm's goals. Managers of small firms emphasized the goal of Employee Welfare more than did managers of larger firms; this finding is in accordance with observations of many writers about the relative advantages of small firms.

Personal value systems do differ in different organizational contexts in ways that are generally understandable. We do not know, however, whether these differences are largely a function of the type of people who go into certain organizational contexts and/or to what extent people's value systems adapt to the organizational context in which they find themselves.

6. There are both differences and similarities in the value systems of managers in the different countries we have studied. We note a similarity of value patterns of managers in countries of diverse social, cultural and technological settings such as the U.S.A., Japan, Korea, India and Australia. One indication of this similarity is seen when we observe the correlation of value patterns between each pair of countries.

	Japan	*Korea*	*India*	*Australia*	*U.S.A.*
Japan		.92	.67	.64	.76
Korea			.71	.64	.72
India				.85	.79
Australia					.95

The correlations show that the value patterns of all the country pairs are significantly related. The U.S.A. and Australia are most similar, Japan and Korea are almost as similar, and India and Australia are quite similar. Korea and Australia, and Japan and Australia are least similar while Japan and India are only slightly more similar. It should be remembered that these are overall country profiles that are being compared and they do not show the individual variation that exists within each country.

Amidst this similarity, there are differences in value patterns between the five countries. A thumbnail sketch of several observations about the values of managers in each country will highlight some of these differences.

U.S.A. Managers

Large element of pragmatism.
Have a high achievement and competence orientation.
Emphasize traditional organizational goals such as Profit Maximization, Organizational Efficiency and High Productivity.
Place high value on most employee groups as significant reference groups.

Japanese Managers

Very high element of pragmatism.
Value magnitude very highly (size and growth).
Place high value on Competence and Achievement.
Have the most homogeneous managerial value system of the countries studied.
Indicate a high degree of value change occurring.

Korean Managers

Large element of pragmatism.
Place low value on most employee groups as significant reference groups.
Display a self-oriented achievement and competence orientation.
Moderate value placed on organizational goals.
Show an intended egalitarian orientation.

Indian Managers

High degree of moralistic orientation.
Value stable organizations with minimal or steady change.
Value personalistic goals and status orientation.
Value a blend of organizational compliance and organizational competence.
Place low value on most employee groups.

Australian Managers

High degree of moralistic orientation.
High level of humanistic orientation.
Place low value on Organizational Growth and Profit Maximization.
Place low value on such concepts as Achievement, Success, Competition and Risk.
Major regional (geographical) differences in values of managers.

7. Our work leads us to the conclusion that the personal values of managers are both measurable and important to measure. Values are related to such practical and important concerns as decision making, managerial success and organizational context differences. While we have learned a great deal about values and their role in organizational life, I am personally struck with how much there is to know. We do not know, for example, how value systems develop and how they are changed by organizational experiences; what are acceptable or optimal levels of value disparity within organizations or suborganizations to aid in the achievement of organizational success; what are the effects upon individuals of providing them with valid information about their own value systems; what values are most compatible with movement toward a post industrial era or multinational corporate life; and finally, how value measurement might aid in the strain toward consistency that all must make between what we believe and value and how be behave. In short, we view the study of value systems and their role in organizational life as an important and on-going venture.

Chapter Two

The Managers Studied

National samples of managers in the United States of America, Japan, Korea, India and Australia were selected from major directories of corporation executives and directors in each respective country. The national samples were developed to be roughly comparable in terms of three stratifying variables: (1) size of organization in terms of number of employees, (2) level of the manager within the organization and (3) organizational function of the manager. The intent of the sample selection procedure was to obtain a diverse group of managers in each country in terms of organizational variables (type of company, size of firm, department or function, organizational level, salary level and line-staff position) and in terms of personal variables (years of managerial experience and age). Tables 2-1 through 2-8 show that the goal of obtaining diverse samples of managers within each country that are comparable from country to country was reasonably met.

The samples come from private as opposed to public (government owned) organizations and represent a large number of organizations. No more than four managers were selected from any one organization. Thus, our results are not heavily influenced by one company's managers.

The number of managers in each country who provided complete information is as follows:

U.S.A.	997
Japan	374
Korea	211
Australia	351
India	623

In total, then, our analyses are based on the responses of these 2556 managers in the five countries. In the U.S.A., Japan, Korea and Australia, the

Table 2-1.   Type of Company in which Managers were Employed

Type of Company	U.S.A. %	Japan %	Korea %	Australia %	India %
Agriculture	2.1	1.0	0.4	2.0	0.3
Mining	0.8	4.3	7.1	2.3	0.6
Construction	1.8	9.6	4.0	5.1	0.8
Manufacturing	56.6	67.8	72.0	42.7	59.7
Transportation and Public Utilities	11.8	5.6	0.9	5.1	1.4
Wholesale and Retail Trade	7.0	2.0	0.9	9.7	11.4
Finance, Insurance and Retail Trade	10.0	4.3	8.0	8.6	3.8
Service	0.7	0.5	0.0	2.6	2.3
Other	8.0	4.9	0.0	21.4	19.7
No Information	1.1	0.0	2.1	1.0	0.0

Table 2-2.   Size of Company in which Managers were Employed

Size of Company*	U.S.A. %	Japan %	Korea %	Australia %	India %
Small	29.0	31.5	48.3	45.3	39.2
Medium	36.2	28.3	26.7	33.3	26.2
Large	33.9	39.8	25.0	21.4	34.6
No Information	0.8	0.4	0.0	0.0	0.0

*The size categories were relative to the individual country and were defined respectively for the U.S.A., Japan, Korea, Australia and India as follows:
  Small—under 500, under 1000, under 500, under 250, under 250
  Medium—500-4999, 1000-4999, 500-999, 250-1999, 250-999
  Large—5000+, 5000+, 1000+, 2000+, 1000+

data was collected by a mail survey. In India, a combined mail and interview approach was used with heavy emphasis on interviewing. Appendix A contains the basic questionnaire used in the five countries. The rate of response to our survey varied by country as follows:

U.S.A.	31 percent
Japan	26 percent
Korea	20 percent
Australia	30 percent
India	72 percent[1]

[1] The relatively high response rate for India was due to the use of interviewing as the primary data collection method.

Table 2-3. Department in which Managers Worked

Department	U.S.A. %	Japan %	Korea %	Australia %	India %
Production	8.2	7.6	12.9	} 12.0	} 9.6
Operations	9.9	2.2	15.6		
Sales-Distribution	9.0	12.7	8.0	12.8	17.0
Engineering	10.3	10.7	8.9	3.1	3.8
Finance-Accounting	6.8	12.2	8.9	9.4	9.7
Personnel-Industrial Relations	15.5	7.9	2.2	6.3	10.3
Public Relations-Advertising	7.5	2.3	0.0	0.0	0.0
Research and Development	11.7	13.2	1.8	2.0	0.0
General Administration	17.0	24.6	34.2	39.0	46.5
Other	3.3	5.6	4.0	14.5	3.1
No Information	1.0	1.0	3.5	0.9	0.0

Table 2-4. Organizational Level of Managers

Organizational Level	U.S.A. %	Japan %	Korea %	Australia %	India %
Top Management[1]	56.6	44.9	57.4	58.4	47.0
Upper Middle Management[2]	30.5	30.7	33.8	25.9	42.6
Lower Middle Management[3]	12.6	6.1	6.3	12.2	9.5
No Information	0.3	18.3	2.5	3.6	0.9

[1] Includes director, president, head of the company, chief executive, senior managing director, managing director, executive vice president, executive manager, general manager, manager of an independent branch, vice president.

[2] Includes level reporting to vice president, department director, general manager of a department, manager of a department, head of a department, works manager, head of a division.

[3] Includes two to four levels below vice president, assistant general manager, plant manager, superintendent, chief of research lab, head of a section, section chief.

Table 2-5. Line-Staff Position of Managers

Type of Position	U.S.A. %	Japan %	Korea %	Australia %	India %
Line Management	26.5	19.8	38.7	32.5	21.1
Staff Management	37.1	33.5	21.3	23.9	31.1
Combined Line-Staff	35.4	45.4	38.7	42.2	47.8
No Information	1.0	1.3	1.3	1.4	0.0

Table 2-6. Salary Level of Managers (Converted to U.S. Dollars)

U.S.A.—Yearly Income		Japan—Yearly Income		Korea—Yearly Income		Australia—Yearly Income		India—Yearly Income	
Under $9,000	4.1%	Under $6,000	19.8%	Under $3,000	76.0%	Under $7,500	8.3%	$800- 1,599	7.2%
9,000-11,999	8.7	6,000- 8,999	27.9	3,000- 5,999	5.3	7,500- 9,999	14.8	1,600- 2,399	11.9
12,000-14,999	12.3	9,000-11,999	17.0	6,000- 8,999	1.8	10,000-12,499	18.2	2,400- 3,199	12.2
15,000-19,999	16.0	12,000-14,999	10.4	9,000-11,999	0.9	12,500-14,999	16.2	3,200- 4,799	26.2
20,000-24,999	15.3	15,000-19,999	10.9	12,000-14,999	1.3	15,000-18,999	14.2	4,800- 6,399	18.9
25,000-34,999	18.1	20,000-24,999	3.8	15,000-24,999	1.3	19,000-24,999	16.5	6,400- 7,999	9.8
35,000-49,000	13.5	25,000-34,999	3.0	25,000-49,999	4.0	25,000 and over	10.5	8,000- 9,599	4.5
50,000 or over	9.6	35,000-49,999	1.5	50,000 or over	2.2			9,600-11,199	2.4
		50,000 or over	4.5					11,200-12,799	3.2
								12,800 and over	2.9
No Information	2.4	No Information	1.2	No Information	7.1	No Information	1.3	No Information	.8

Table 2-7.   Years of Managerial Experience

Years of Managerial Experience	U.S.A. %	Japan %	Korea %	Australia %	India %
0-5	17.7	26.1	0.9	10.7	18.3
6-10	20.6	24.6	38.7	16.0	30.4
11-15	21.1	18.3	22.2	24.2	24.9
16-20	18.4	16.2	3.6	17.1	12.8
21-30	14.1	12.9	4.4	19.7	9.3
Over 30	6.3	2.1	1.8	12.0	4.3
No information	1.8	0.3	28.4	2.8	0.0

Table 2-8.   Age of Managers

Age in Years	U.S.A. %	Japan %	Korea %	Australia %	India %
20-29	2.6	0.0	4.9	3.7	5.3
30-39	18.9	2.3*	25.3	18.5	34.2
40-49	37.2	18.5	44.4	38.5	38.9
50-59	29.0	66.2	18.2	29.9	17.9
60 and over	11.8	12.4	4.4	9.4	3.7
No Information	0.6	0.6	2.8	0.0	0.0

*The lack of young managers in Japan reflects the slow career advancement in Japan. Yoshino (1968) notes: "Although there is some variance among firms, the general rule is that one must be with the company for at least 8 to 10 years before being promoted to the rank of subsection chief. It takes another several years before one is ready to become the chief of a section—the first managerial position of any significance. Fifteen to 20 years of seniority are required before one is promoted to the position of deputy department manager or its equivalent."

While stratified random sampling from a national roster was used in each country, the rate of returns make it difficult to claim the samples as truly representative. It seems clear, however, that our samples are sufficiently representative of each country's managers and are sufficiently comparable from country to country to permit the analyses presented in the following chapters.

In summary, we are dealing with over 2500 top and middle management managers from a variety of industries. The managers come from organizations of all sizes and represent major functional areas of management. The managers are an experienced group; the average number of years spent in a management position is about 15 years while the average age in our total sample is about 45 years.

Chapter Three

Comparative Analysis of Values Held by Managers in Five Countries

The present chapter focuses on questions concerning the similarity and differences in personal value systems of managers in the five countries. We are interested in the extent of similarities and differences among the countries and in the nature of these similarities and differences.

PRIMARY ORIENTATIONS IN THE FIVE COUNTRIES

The first comparison of values among managers in the five countries is in terms of primary orientations. Each manager is classified into one of four primary orientation groups: *pragmatic, moralistic, affective* and *mixed*. A manager is classified into one of these primary value orientations on the basis of his evaluations of the 66 concepts in the PVQ. The essential purpose of this classification is to provide a means of eliminating some of the intentionality of values and getting closer to values that are behaviorally relevant.

Pragmatists are those managers who generally characterize the concepts they view as high in importance as successful. Their evaluation of importance is based on pragmatic considerations of whether or not something will work, will it be successful or not. As indicated earlier, this pragmatic orientation is commonly suggested in management literature and we would expect it to be a major orientation of managers.

Moralistically oriented managers are those who characterize the concepts they see as high in importance as right. Their evaluation of importance is based on concerns of right or wrong and suggests a moral, ethical or normative value orientation. We would expect the moralistic orientation to be importantly represented in our samples of managers.

Affectively oriented managers characterize concepts they see as high in importance as pleasant. Their evaluation of importance is based on hedonism and suggests a feeling or affect orientation. We would anticipate that the affect orientation would be less frequent for managers than either the pragmatic or moralistic orientations.

If a manager clearly cannot be placed in one of the preceding orientations, we classify him into a mixed value orientation category.

As seen in Table 3-1, combining managers from all countries (international sample) shows slightly over one-half to be pragmatists, about one-fourth to be moralists, only about one-twentieth to be affect-oriented and slightly more than one-sixth to have mixed orientations. The relative size of these proportions is roughly comparable to what one would expect from reading the general literature on orientations of managers.

There are major differences in the orientations among the different countries. Japanese managers are pragmatically oriented to the greatest degree, U.S. and Korean managers are next in pragmatic orientation, while Indian and Australian managers are least pragmatically oriented. The extent of these differences in pragmatic orientation is quite large; a ratio of about two to one for Japanese as compared to Indian managers.

There are also rather large differences in moralistic orientations among managers in the five countries. Indian and Australian managers are moralistically oriented to the greatest degree, U.S. managers are next, while Japanese and Korean managers have relatively low moralistic orientations. Again, the magnitude of the differences between countries is rather large.

The affective orientation is a minor orientation for managers from each country; less than 10 percent of managers in any country being so classified.

The proportion of managers that we classify as having mixed orientations are relatively similar across the five countries with the exception of

Table 3-1. Primary Orientations of Managers in the Five Countries (Percent)

Country	Pragmatic	Moralistic	Affective	Mixed	Total N
Japan	67.4	9.9	7.0	15.8	374
U.S.A.	57.3	30.3	1.2	11.2	997
Korea	53.1	9.0	8.5	29.4	211
Australia	40.2	40.2	5.4	14.2	351
India	34.0	44.1	2.2	19.6	623
International Sample*	52.9	24.4	5.1	17.6	750

*The international sample is composed of a random sample of 150 managers drawn from each country sample. This international sample is used as a reference group against which each country can be compared.

Korean managers. While we are not certain as to the reason for Korea being relatively high in the mixed orientation category, we suspect that it indicates that personal orientations are more individualistic in Korea and that there is less of a national pattern than is the case for managers in the other countries.

In terms of primary orientations, Japanese and Indian managers are most *dissimilar* while Indian and Australian managers are most *similar*. While it is tempting to make behavioral inferences directly from a manager's primary value orientation (e.g., moralists behave more ethically, affect-oriented managers engage in more hedonistic behavior), it should be remembered that primary value orientation classification is only a means to help determine which concepts are more behaviorally relevant for an individual. It is only when individuals (or groups) have different value profiles (i.e., different concepts comprise operative value sets) that we would expect behavioral differences. Thus two individuals (or groups) having different primary value orientations need not be expected to behave differently. By the same logic, individuals (or groups) with identical primary value orientations need not be expected to behave similarly. The crucial thing is whether or not the comparison individuals or groups have different value profiles. It can be noted here that different primary value orientations are indeed associated with different value profiles; a detailed presentation of these results, however, is more appropriately dealt with in Chapter Six.

INTERNATIONAL VALUE PROFILE

An individual value profile can be constructed for each manager by utilizing his primary value orientation and the importance he attaches to the concepts in the PVQ. This value profile allows interpretation of an individual's responses to the 66 concepts in the PVQ in value terms which have behavioral implications. The value profile utilizes four categories of values: operative, intended, adopted and weak values. Operative values are those concepts which are rated as "high importance" by a manager and fit his primary value orientation. For a pragmatic manager, this would include those concepts which he jointly considers as "high importance" and "successful." Similarly, "high importance-right" and "high importance-pleasant" combinations would define operative values for persons with moralistic and affect value orientations, respectively. In terms of implications for behavior, operative values are likely to be the most influential.

Intended values are those concepts which an individual regards as being of high importance but which seem not to fit his organizational experience. These values seem generally to be socioculturally induced. For a pragmatic individual, intended values would be all those concepts which are rated by him as "high importance" and "right" or "pleasant." In the same way, "high importance-successful/pleasant" ratings would yield intended values for moralistic individuals and "high importance-successful/right" ratings would yield intended values for affect-oriented individuals. Intended values may imply a conflict between what one has come to believe and what one sees functioning or rewarded in his organizational environment. Intended values are thus viewed as influencing one's behavior to a lesser extent than do operative values.

Adopted values are those concepts which fit the primary value orientation of an individual but which he does not regard as being highly important. Such values seem situationally induced in that, while they are borne out by an individual's organizational experience, he finds them difficult to internalize. For a pragmatically oriented individual, adopted values consist of those concepts which are rated by him as "successful" and of either "average importance" or "low importance." Similarly, for a moralistic or an affective individual, adopted values would be shown by "right-average/low importance" or "pleasant-average/low importance" ratings, respectively. Adopted values are expected to exercise less influence on one's behavior than either operative or intended values.

Weak values are the remaining set of concepts which are regarded as neither highly important nor fitting the primary value orientation of the individual. These would be comprised of concepts rated as "average-low importance" and "right-pleasant" for a pragmatic individual; "average-low importance" and "successful-pleasant" for a moralistic person; and "average-low importance" and "successful-right" for an effectively oriented individual. Weak values are not expected to influence an individual's behavior to any large extent.

Given the preceding definitions of the four categories of values, an individual's value profile can be constructed by listing those concepts in the PVQ which for him are operative values, intended values, adopted values and weak values. Such a value profile can be constructed for each manager in each country, excluding those managers who have a mixed value orientation. This exclusion is necessary because the probability scores used in the classification procedure cannot be computed for a manager with a mixed value orientation.

Rokeach (1968) has developed the notions of centrality-peripheralness to interpret behaviorally one's belief or value systems. He argues and presents some data indicating that beliefs can be arranged in terms of their centralness or peripheralness to a person. The more central a belief is to a person, the more stable the belief, the more resistant it is to change and the wider the domain is over which it exercises influence. Our view of the behavioral relevance of different types of values is similar and could be diagrammed as shown in Figure 3-1.

The concepts making up an individual's operative values are viewed as most central to him and have the greatest impact on his behavior. Concepts making up an individual's intended values and adopted values are respectively less central to him and would be expected to have decreasing general influence on his behavior. Those concepts forming a person's weak values are least central (most peripheral) to him and would not be expected to influence his behavior to any great extent.

It is also possible to derive an overall value profile for any group of managers (for example, managers in each country) by aggregating all of the relevant individual value profiles. For this purpose, a matrix can be prepared for each concept. For example, if we are interested in considering the concept High Productivity for the international sample of managers, the matrix shown as Figure 3-2 would result.

This matrix shows that the concept High Productivity is an operative value for 68 percent, an intended value for 18 percent, an adopted value for 6 percent and a weak value for 8 percent of the international sample of managers. The overall value profile for the international sample would show a similar categorization for each of the 66 concepts in the PVQ. While this data display (as presented in Appendix B) is most complete, it is somewhat difficult to interpret comparatively because of its voluminous nature (66 concepts x 4 value types x 5 countries). Therefore, two derived summary indexes have been used to portray value patterns and their behavioral relevance. The first behavioral relevance score is generated by utilizing a weighting scheme for all of the 66 concepts which weights the four value categories in descending order from operative values to weak values in terms of behavioral relevance. The simplest such weighting scheme would give a weight of three to operative values, a weight of two to intended values, a weight of one to adopted values and a weight of zero to weak values. When this weighting scheme is applied to a concept and divided by three it establishes a behavioral relevance score which can range from zero to 100. Using the concept of High Productivity for the international sample as an example, this scoring procedure can be illustrated:

$$
\begin{aligned}
\text{Behavioral Relevance Score for High Productivity} &= \frac{3 \text{ (operative value score)} + 2 \text{ (intended value score)} + 1 \text{ (adopted value score)}}{3} \\
&= \frac{3 \, (68) + 2 \, (18) + 1 \, (6)}{3} \\
&= 82
\end{aligned}
$$

The second behavioral relevance score emphasizes only operative values and is simply the percentage of the total group for whom the concept is an operative value. This score can also vary between zero and 100 for any given concept. For the concept High Productivity for the international sample, this score would be 68 since 68 percent of the international sample viewed it as an operative value.

These two scoring methods are highly correlated (.97 to .99 for each country sample) and in a relative sense it makes little difference which

Figure 3-1. Behavioral Relevance of Different Types of Values

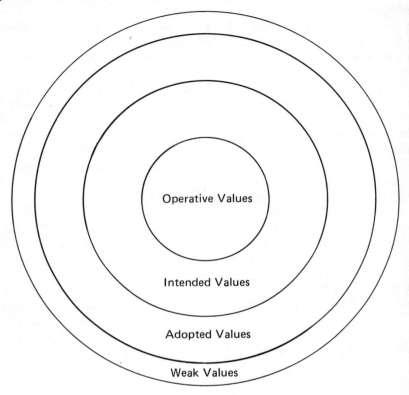

Figure 3-2. Matrix for Concept High Productivity for International Sample of Managers

	High Importance (HI)	Average-Low Importance ($\overline{HI}$)
Primary Orientation (PO)	.68	.06
Not Primary Orientation ($\overline{PO}$)	.18	.08
		1.00

one is used to present group results. We have chosen the latter score to present here since it is the simplest and most easily understood.

Figure 3-3 represents a useful way of viewing the overall value profile for the international sample of managers as a group by showing the operative value scores for each concept in the five content groupings of concepts. It should be remembered that the higher the operative value score, the greater the behavioral relevance of the concept for the managers.

With respect to the *organizational goal* concepts, it can be seen that these eight concepts constitute three subsets of goals. The first subset includes the goals High Productivity and Organizational Efficiency. For the international sample of managers, these seem to be what Simon (1964) calls maximization criteria. They (productivity and efficiency) are the primary goals which managers attempt to influence by their actions, decisions and behavior and are useful in generating alternative courses of action or ways of behaving.

A second subset of *organizational goals* consists of Organizational Growth, Profit Maximization, Organizational Stability, Industry Leadership and Employee Welfare. The secondary position of these goals in terms of behavioral relevance and their content would suggest that they be viewed as expected consequences of the maximization criteria. It is through productivity and efficiency that the goals of growth, stability, profit, industry leadership and employee welfare are to be achieved. A related way of looking at the first two subsets of organizational goals would be in terms of means-ends distinctions. Productivity and efficiency are the means while growth, profit, stability, leadership and employee welfare are the end goals. It is interesting to note that the means goals have higher behavioral relevance than do the end goals for this international sample of managers. It seems that the means are perceived as so vital that they tend to overshadow the ends in terms of behavioral relevance. Logically, this should not be the case, but behaviorally, it seems to be the case; managers after all are pragmatic beings.

The final subset of *organizational goals* includes only Social Welfare which is viewed as an operative value by only 16 percent of the sample while 53 percent view it as a weak value. Therefore, it would be expected to have relatively little impact on managers' behavior unless outside pressures (such as social legislation) forced such concerns.

Concepts dealing with *personal goals of individuals* form two distinct subsets of personal goals. Achievement, Creativity, Success and Job Satisfaction are the personal goals that represent high level operative values for this international sample of managers. It is suggested that these concepts are the keystones in the motivational structure underlying managerial behavior. It is through achievement, creativity, success and job satisfaction that managers see their personal goals and ambitions realized. Again, one is struck by the fact that these are essentially means goals and that means tend to overshadow ends.

The second subset of personal goals has much lower behavioral relevance scores and is made up of intended, adopted and weak values.

Figure 3-3.   Value Profile for International Sample of Managers

BEHAVIORAL RELEVANCE SCORE	ORGANIZATIONAL GOALS	PERSONAL GOALS	GROUPS OF PEOPLE	IDEAS ASSOCIATED WITH PEOPLE	GENERAL TOPICS
70	High Productivity				
	Organizational Efficiency	Achievement	My Company	Ability	
60		Creativity	Customers	Skill	
		Success	Technical Employees		
			Managers	Cooperation	
50	Organizational Growth	Job Satisfaction	My Subordinates	Trust	
	Profit Maximization				
	Organizational Stability		Me	Ambition	Competition
			Craftsmen	Loyalty	Rational
40	Industry Leadership		My Boss	Aggressiveness	
	Employee Welfare			Honor	
			My Co-workers		
30		Autonomy	Owners		Authority
		Security	White Collar Employees		Property
		Individuality	Blue Collar Workers		

20

10

Social Welfare

Dignity	Stockholders Government	Tolerance Obedience	Caution Change Risk Force Compromise Liberalism Equality
Money			
Influence	Labor Unions		
Prestige	Laborers		
		Compassion	Religion
Power			Emotions
Leisure		Conformity	
			Conservatism
		Prejudice	Conflict

These results are highly consistent with those reported by Haire, Ghiselli and Porter (1966) in their study of 3600 managers in 14 countries. They studied the importance of various types of needs of managers by using a modified version of Maslow's need classification system. Table 3-2 shows the relative importance of each need category across the 3600 managers in their study and a categorization of the personal goal concepts in the PVQ into each need category.

The present results are generally similar to those reported by Haire et al. and underscore the extreme importance of self-actualization needs or goals in the motivational structure of managers.

With respect to *groups of people* and institutions, the set of concepts including My Company, Customers, Technical Employees and Managers represent operative values for these managers and are significant reference groups in shaping manager behavior. A second set of concepts including My Subordinates, Employees, Me, Craftsmen and My Boss represent a second level of values that are largely intended values.

With respect to *ideas associated with people*, Ability, Skill and Cooperation are operative values while Trust, Ambition, Loyalty, Aggressiveness and Honor have moderate behavioral relevance scores and are intended and adopted values. These two sets of characteristics would be expected to influence a manager's behavior as well as the way in which he judges and evaluates others. The first set of concepts would seem to represent a competence dimension while the second set represents an organizational compliance dimension. Both dimensions are obviously a part of the manager's value system.

Table 3-2. Comparison of Haire Data with PVQ Results

Need Category	Importance of Need Areas in Haire Data	PVQ Concepts Assigned to Need Categories	Average Behavioral Relevance Score
Security	5.74*	Security Money	26.0
Social	5.37	−	−
Esteem	5.26	Dignity Prestige Power	17.3
Autonomy	5.90	Autonomy Individuality Influence	25.5
Self-actualization	6.25	Achievement Creativity Success Job Satisfaction	59.6

*High scores represent high importance needs.

With respect to *ideas about general topics*, no concept is an operative value for at least half the managers. The concepts Competition and Rational are adopted and intended values respectively and have behavior relevance scores of 46 and 43.

The value profile for the international sample of managers as shown in Figure 3-3 presents an overall view of the 66 concepts and their role in the value structure of managers which can be interpreted behaviorally.

VALUE PROFILE DIFFERENCES AMONG THE FIVE COUNTRIES

The personal value systems of national samples of American, Japanese, Korean, Indian and Australian managers have been assessed through the use of a standard theoretical and measurement approach and are aggregated to present country comparisons in this section. It should again be noted that in the case of the Japanese and Korean studies, the PVQ was translated into their language through translation and back-translation techniques but comparisons may lose some interpretability because of translation problems. In the case of U.S.A., India and Australia, the same English language version of the PVQ was used and translation problems are not a factor. The five country studies are also subject to an ethnocentricity bias with regard to selection of the concepts that make up the PVQ. The concepts were selected to be a relevant set of value concepts for American managers and were developed largely out of American literature. If one grants that they are a relevant set of concepts for American managers, there is no guarantee that they will be equally relevant for managers from other countries. We have not systematically dealt with this problem and can only report what we have found and be cautious about our interpretations.

Tables 3-3 through 3-7 present the operative value scores for each group of concepts for each national sample of managers and for the international sample. Again, it should be remembered that the higher the operative value score for a concept, the greater the behavioral relevance of the concept.

From Table 3-3, it can be seen that there are 16 significant differences on organizational goal concepts out of a possible 40 (8 concepts x 5 countries). These differences involve all organizational goal concepts with the exception of Social Welfare and involve all countries except the United States. The first major difference among the five countries is that Japanese managers attach greater relevance to organizational goals as a group and specifically to High Productivity, Organizational Growth, Profit Maximization, Organizational Stability and Industry Leadership. This would imply that the goals of organizations are more internalized in the value structure of Japanese managers and would be expected to influence their behavior to a greater extent than is the case in the other countries. The relatively low relevance placed by Japanese managers on Employee Welfare seems contrary to what would be expected from reading

Japanese employee relations literature. Our data suggest, however, that Employee Welfare is a very high level intended value for Japanese managers (an intended value score of 60 as compared to 38 for the international sample) and as such it represents a high level of intentionality that does not get fully translated into behavior.

A second difference among the five countries is the lower relevance placed on organizational goals as a group by Korean managers, specifically on Organizational Efficiency, Industry Leadership and Employee Welfare. These include both means and end goals and imply a low level of internalization of organizational goals in the value structure of Korean managers with the accompanying lowered behavioral impact. The goal Organizational Growth is highly valued by Korean managers relative to other countries and probably represents a strong desire for continued industrial development by Korean managers.

The third difference noted among the five countries involves the relatively low relevance placed on the organizational goals Organizational Growth and Profit Maximization by Australian managers. Profit and particularly growth are not highly internalized as a part of the value structure of Australian managers. Australian managers do place relatively high value on Employee Welfare and Social Welfare (although Social Welfare does not quite meet our

Table 3-3. Country Comparisons—Organizational Goals

Concept	International Sample N=618*	U.S.A. N=885	Japan N=315	Korea N=149	Australia N=301	India N=501
High Productivity	68	63	(79)**	67	62	62
Organizational Efficiency	64	65	62	(49)	64	69
Organizational Growth	51	50	(72)	(61)	(29)	47
Profit Maximization	49	58	(61)	45	(38)	(36)
Organizational Stability	46	41	(58)	55	41	(58)
Industry Leadership	40	43	(50)	(30)	44	38
Employee Welfare	34	34	(21)	(20)	(45)	(44)
Social Welfare	16	8	11	14	25	18

*These samples are smaller than those reported earlier because managers with mixed orientations are excluded from this analysis.

**Operative value scores are circled for any country when they deviate from the international sample by 10 percent or greater. This 10 percent difference is both statistically and practically significant.

difference criterion); this is consistent with a pattern of humanistic orientation for Australian managers which is later developed as we look at more data.

The final difference among the five countries on organizational goal concepts involves the relatively high value placed by Indian managers on Organizational Stability and the relatively low value placed on Profit Maximization. Both of these results seem consistent with a heavily planned economy such as is present in India. The relatively high value placed on Employee Welfare by Indian managers is inconsistent with later data reported which shows that *groups of people* do not play as significant a part in the value system of Indian managers as is generally the case in the other countries. One can speculate that the present result on Employee Welfare represents managerial awareness of the importance of labor-intensive efforts to aid in Indian employment problems.

In summary, it seems clear that there are differences among the countries on most organizational goals. These differences are most frequent in the case of Japan and least frequent in the United States. Organizational goals make up 12 percent of the concepts in the PVQ but are involved in 17 percent of the country differences found on the 66 concepts. Organizational goals, then, are a set of concepts where country differences occur frequently in both absolute and relative terms.

Table 3-4 presents the five country data for personal *goals of individuals.* There are 20 significant differences out of a possible 65 (13 concepts x 5 countries). These differences involve all *personal* goals except Influence and Leisure and involve all five countries. The first major difference among the five countries is the high relevance attached to personal goals by Indian managers generally and specifically on Job Satisfaction, Security, Individuality, Dignity, Prestige and Power. This suggests that personal goals play an important part in the value structure of Indian managers and a high level of personalism seems evident for Indian managers. This finding of a high degree of personalism for Indian managers is consistent with Chowdhry's observations about managing agencies which established most modern industry in India: "The typical organization of a managing agency can be described as highly centralized and personal, with a rigid social structure" (Chowdhry, 1970). Job Satisfaction, Security and Individuality would seem to represent intrinsically desirable personal goals while Dignity, Prestige and Power seem to represent status and/or ascribed personal goals. Indian managers attach high relevance to both types of personal goals and both certainly seem a part of the value system of Indian managers.

A second observation about personal goals is that U.S. and Australian managers generally attach less relevance to them than is the case in the other countries. This is particularly so on Creativity, Success and Autonomy for Australian managers and on Autonomy and Security for American managers.

Finally, the nature of the personal goals sought by Japanese and Korean managers are somewhat different. Japanese managers give relatively greater value to Achievement, Creativity and Autonomy.

Table 3-4.   Country Comparisons—Personal Goals of Individuals

Concept	International Sample	U.S.A.	Japan	Korea	Australia	India
Achievement	62	63	(77)	60	55	65
Creativity	60	53	(73)	(73)	(44)	60
Success	56	52	58	64	(40)	57
Job Satisfaction	50	51	(34)	45	54	(68)
Autonomy	30	(13)	(44)	(55)	(16)	25
Security	29	(15)	26	35	28	(40)
Individuality	28	33	23	33	33	(38)
Dignity	26	30	(9)	(16)	28	(49)
Money	23	19	19	(35)	18	22
Influence	18	12	26	26	12	18
Prestige	16	11	13	10	10	(41)
Power	10	6	9	16	6	(21)
Leisure	6	3	3	12	6	10

To summarize, there are differences in personal goals among the five countries. Indian managers place the greatest relevance on personal goals while Australian and American managers place the least relevance on them. Personal goals make up 20 percent of the concepts in the PVQ and are involved in 21 percent of the country differences found on the 66 concepts.

Table 3-5 presents the five country results for concepts dealing with *groups of people and institutions.* There are 20 significant differences out of a possible 85 (17 concepts x 5 countries). These differences involve all five countries and about three-fourths of the concepts. The most striking observation from Table 3-5 is that *groups of people* play a much more significant part in the value system of American managers and a much less significant part in the value system of Indian managers. Specifically, American managers place relatively high relevance on Customers, Owners, Stockholders, My Boss, Employees and My Co-workers. Indian managers place relatively low relevance on Managers, Employees, My Subordinates, White Collar Employees and Blue Collar Workers. This finding of relatively low relevancy of groups of workers to Indian managers also has been found in other studies using different samples and measurement approaches (Haire et al., 1966; Smith and Thomas, 1972; Negandhi and Prasad, 1971).

Japanese managers value Technical Employees highly; Australian managers value Employees and My Subordinates highly, while Korean managers are closest to the Indian pattern of attaching low relevance to groups of people.

In summary, the major difference between the countries on concepts

Table 3-5. Country Comparisons—Groups of People and Institutions

Concept	International Sample	U.S.A.	Japan	Korea	Australia	India
My Company	61	69	61	53	63	57
Customers	61	⑦①	63	④⑦	67	61
Technical Employees	57	51	⑥⑦	53	50	56
Managers	56	59	63	57	51	④③
My Subordinates	50	56	50	④⓪	⑥⓪	④⓪
Employees*	45	⑥⓪	44	38	⑤⑦	③④
Me	41	47	40	42	42	32
Craftsmen*	41	38	38	42	42	49
My Boss	38	⑤④	33	30	37	41
My Co-workers	30	④③	①⑦	22	39	33
Owners	29	③⑨	①⑥	26	27	27
White Collar Employees	28	35	23	22	29	①②
Blue Collar Workers*	27	28	30	33	28	①②
Stockholders	25	③⑦	24	21	24	23
Government	25	25	①②	25	31	33
Labor Unions	19	14	17	15	26	25
Laborers*	16	22	⑤	9	24	9

*In the Indian PVQ these concepts were: Technical Staff, Highly Skilled Workers, All Employees, Semiskilled Workers and Unskilled Workers respectively.

dealing with *groups of people and institutions* is between American and Indian managers, with American managers placing high relevance on such groups and Indian managers placing low relevance on them. Concepts dealing with groups of people make up 26 percent of the concepts in the PVQ but are involved in only 20 percent of the country differences found on the 66 concepts.

Table 3-6 presents the five country results for concepts dealing with *ideas associated with people.* There are 22 significant differences out of a possible 65 (13 concepts x 5 countries). These differences involve all five countries but only about 60 percent of the concepts. The first observation from Table 3-6 is that Australian managers place relatively high relevance on Honor, Loyalty, Trust, Tolerance and Compassion. This suggests a rather high level of humanistic orientation and is consistent with the earlier finding that Australian managers value Employee Welfare and Social Welfare to a relatively high degree.

Indian managers score relatively high on the concepts Obedience, Loyalty, Trust and Honor, suggesting an organizational compliance orientation.

Table 3-6. Country Comparisons—Ideas Associated with People

Concept	International Sample	U.S.A.	Japan	Korea	Australia	India
Ability	67	65	73	68	64	65
Skill	58	55	60	50	65	61
Cooperation	55	53	49	56	60	57
Trust	50	46	(34)	52	(60)	(62)
Ambition	43	(58)	(26)	39	46	49
Loyalty	40	43	(11)	(25)	(55)	(60)
Aggressiveness	34	35	(55)	(50)	(11)	(16)
Honor	32	41	(12)	(20)	(53)	(43)
Tolerance	23	22	(12)	18	(35)	28
Obedience	21	18	(3)	15	24	(44)
Compassion	13	16	5	10	(25)	12
Conformity	9	2	8	16	3	16
Prejudice	4	4	2	7	3	3

Both Indian and Australian managers reject the notion of Aggressiveness as being behaviorally relevant. This result is compatible with the humanistic orientation suggested for Australian managers and the organizational compliance orientation suggested for Indian managers.

Japanese managers score very low on the concepts Loyalty, Honor, Trust, Tolerance and Obedience which suggests a very low level of humanistic orientation and/or organizational compliance orientation. This finding with respect to placing low value on Loyalty and Obedience is particularly surprising since these concepts are often reported as being important facets in the Japanese value system. Several different ways of looking at our data, however, show that Japanese managers do indeed place low value on these concepts and we are inclined to accept this evidence. Both Japanese and Korean managers place relatively high value on the concept of Aggressiveness, just the opposite of the case for Australian and Indian managers.

Korean and American managers are involved in only a few of the country differences. American managers place relatively high value on Ambition and Korean managers place relatively low value on Loyalty and Honor.

In summary, it is suggested that Australian managers show a high humanistic orientation, Indian managers show an organizational compliance orientation, while Japanese managers are low on both of these types of orientations. Concepts dealing with ideas associated with people comprise 20 percent of the concepts in the PVQ but are involved in 24 percent of the country differences found on the 66 concepts.

Table 3-7 presents the five country results for the concepts relating

Table 3-7. Country Comparisons—Ideas About General Topics

Concept	International Sample	U.S.A.	Japan	Korea	Australia	India
Competition	46	48	47	37	38	44
Rational	43	37	⑤④	41	38	40
Authority	27	29	①④	26	26	34
Property	26	31	25	㉟	17	⑮
Caution	24	⑨	㊼	㊵	⑧	26
Change	24	㉞	22	⑬	28	18
Risk	22	28	17	⑧	18	28
Force	18	⑥	㊴	㉜	③	⑦
Compromise	17	13	11	㉗	14	15
Liberalism	16	⑥	14	22	21	20
Equality	15	16	10	15	17	21
Religion	12	19	3	9	12	11
Emotions	8	12	4	9	14	5
Conservatism	5	9	1	5	3	3
Conflict	5	6	1	5	5	6

to *ideas about general topics*. There are 18 significant differences out of a possible 75 (15 concepts x 5 countries). These differences involve all five countries and occur on 60 percent of the concepts. It should be noted that *general topics* do not play as important a role in the value structure of managers in all five countries as do the other groups of concepts. Notwithstanding this, several observations can be made. American managers value Change relatively highly and value Caution to a low degree. This suggests an active or dynamic orientation. Japanese managers, however, value Caution and Rational to a relatively high degree which implies a highly rationalized and cautious style of behavior. This finding is certainly in accord with the highly rationalized and consential type of decision making that has been reported for Japanese managers by many observers (Yoshino, 1968; Abegglen, 1973; Ballon, 1969).

Korean managers value Caution, Force and Compromise relatively highly and value Risk and Change to a relatively low degree. This suggests a cautious and static strategy in behaving which requires a high degree of accommodation or compromise in achieving desired outcomes.

In summary, it is suggested that American managers display an active or dynamic orientation in their value systems, Japanese managers display a cautious rationality in their value systems, while Korean managers display a cautious accommodation orientation in their value systems. Concepts dealing with general topics comprise 23 percent of the concepts in the PVQ but are involved in only 19 percent of the country differences found on the 66 concepts.

Table 3-8 presents a summary of the differences for each country for each group of concepts. Japanese managers are involved in a relatively high number of differences (27) while U.S. managers are involved in a relatively low number of differences (13). The set of concepts dealing with organizational goals is involved in a relatively high proportion of the differences (40 percent) while concepts dealing with groups of people and general topics are involved in a relatively lower proportion of the differences (24 percent). The fact that significant differences were found on 29 percent of the possible concept-country combinations is strong evidence that there are meaningful differences between the countries in terms of their value systems.

Table 3-9 shows the content of the differences found between the five countries when each country is compared to the international sample of managers. Major observations from Table 3-9 are as follows:

U.S.A.

High level of orientation toward groups of people as a relevant part of the value structure.

Japan

High level of internalization of organizational goals.
High level of rationality orientation.
Low level of humanistic and organizational compliance orientation.

Korea

High accommodation and/or compromise orientation coupled with a low change orientation.
Low level of humanistic orientation.

Australia

Very high level of humanistic orientation.
Low level of personal and organizational competence orientation.

India

High level of personalistic orientation.
High level of organizational compliance orientation.
Low level of orientation toward groups of people as a relevant part of the value structure.

A final way of showing the concept similarities and differences between the five countries is by ranking the operative value scores on the 66 concepts for each country and by correlating these five sets of ranks with each other. Table 3-10 shows the resulting intercountry correlations from this procedure. These correlations show that the value patterns of all the country

Table 3-8. Differences by Country in Operative Value Scores on Groups of Concepts

Concept Groups	*U.S.A.*	*Japan*	*Korea*	*Australia*	*India*	*Total Number of Differences*	*Percent of Total Possible Differences*
Organizational Goals	0	6	4	3	3	16	40
Personal Goals	2	5	4	3	6	20	31
Groups of People	6	5	2	2	5	20	24
Characteristics of Individuals	1	7	3	6	5	22	34
General Topics	4	4	6	2	2	18	24
Total Number of Differences	13	27	19	16	21	96	
Percent of Total Possible Differences	14	28	20	17	22		29

Table 3-9.   Country Comparisons—High and Low Operative Value Scores

HIGH SCORES

U.S.A.	Japan	Korea	Australia	India
My Boss	Organizational Growth	Caution	Honor	Prestige
Employees	Profit Maximization	Force	Loyalty	Dignity
My Co-workers	Organizational Stability	Property	Trust	Power
Stockholders	High Productivity	Compromise	Compassion	Job Satisfaction
Owners	Industry Leadership		Tolerance	Security
Customers		Autonomy		Individuality
	Achievement	Creativity	Employees	
Ambition	Creativity	Money	My Subordinates	Obedience
	Autonomy			Loyalty
Change	Caution	Aggressiveness	Employee Welfare	Trust
	Rational			Honor
	Force	Organizational Growth		
	Technical Employees			Employee Welfare
	Agressiveness			Organizational Stability

LOW SCORES

U.S.A.	Japan	Korea	Australia	India
Autonomy	Loyalty	Organizational Efficiency	Organizational Growth	Managers
Security	Honor	Industry Leadership		White Collar Employees
	Trust		Profit Maximization	Blue Collar Workers
Caution	Obedience	Employee Welfare		Employees
	Dignity		Aggressiveness	My Subordinates
Force	Tolerance	Customers	Success	
Liberalism	Ambition	My Subordinates	Creativity	Aggressiveness
			Autonomy	Force
Employee Welfare		Loyalty		Property
My Co-workers		Honor	Caution	

Laborers

Owners

Government

Job Satisfaction

Authority

Dignity

Risk

Change

Force

Profit Maximization

Table 3-10.   Intercorrelations Between Countries on Ranked
Concept Operative Value Scores

	Japan	*Korea*	*India*	*Australia*	*U.S.A.*
Japan		.92	.67	.64	.76
Korea			.71	.64	.72
India				.85	.79
Australia					.95

pairs are significantly and positively related. The United States and Australia are most similar, Japan and Korea are almost as similar, and India and Australia are quite similar. Korea and Australia, and Japan and Australia are least similar, while Japan and India are only slightly more similar. It should be remembered that we are correlating overall country profiles (essentially average profiles) and the correlation of average measures usually results in relatively high correlations. These figures certainly mask the individual variability that is found within each country.

RELATIVE VARIABILITY OF MANAGERIAL
VALUE SYSTEMS WITHIN THE
FIVE COUNTRIES

The question of whether or not managers in any given country have more homogeneous value systems than is the case in other countries is addressed in this section. One might expect, for example, that Japanese managers would have relatively homogeneous value systems because there is but one language and one ethnic group involved, because the relatively dense population would effectively transmit and reinforce a given value structure, and because of the relative isolation of Japan from other countries during long periods of her history. All of these factors would argue for the expectation that Japanese managers would have homogeneous value systems. At the other extreme, one would expect Indian managers to have less homogeneous value systems because of major language differences, major regional ethnic composition differences, and because of the mixed capitalistic and socialistic governmental structure under which Indian managers function.

To test these expectations, we have created a deviation measure for each of the 66 concepts for each country. The deviation measure essentially gets at meaning similarity of responses to each concept by the managers from a given country. To illustrate the procedure, consider the value type responses of American managers to the concept Caution.

Caution (American Managers)

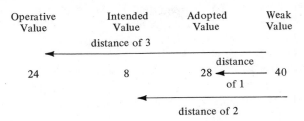

For American managers, Caution is an operative value for 24 percent, an intended value for 8 percent, an adopted value for 28 percent and a weak value for 40 percent. To obtain a deviation measure for this concept, we select that value type which contains the highest percentage of managers and compute weighted differences from this modal response category.

$$\text{Average Deviation Score} = (1 \times .28) + (2 \times .08) + (3 \times .24)$$

$$= 1.16$$

Another example would be shown by the concept Employee Welfare for American managers.

Employee Welfare (American Managers)

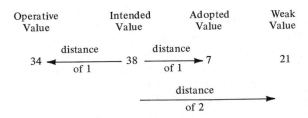

The modal response is intended value so differences are weighted from this response category.

$$\text{AD Score (Employee Welfare)} = (1 \times .34) + (1 \times .07) + (2 \times .21)$$

$$= .83$$

This score can vary from zero (if 100 percent of the responses were of one value type) to 1.65 (if the response split were 34 percent, 0 percent, 33 percent, 33 percent for the value types respectively). Empirically, among the five samples the least variable concept has an AD score of 0.13 and the most variable concept has an AD score of 1.63.

Table 3-11 shows the Average Deviation Score for the twenty-fifth percentile (P 25), the fiftieth percentile (P 50), and the seventy-fifth percentile (P 75) on the 66 concepts for each country. It should be remembered that low scores indicate homogeneous value systems and high scores indicate heterogeneous value systems.

As expected, Japan has the lowest deviation scores and clearly have the most homogeneous value system of any of the five countries. The United States is second in homogeneity, while Australia and India are third and fourth respectively in homogeneity of value systems. Korea is the least homogeneous (most heterogeneous) country in terms of managerial value systems.

FACTOR STRUCTURE OF THE VALUE SYSTEMS OF MANAGERS IN THE FIVE COUNTRIES

The final method of looking at similarities and differences in managerial value systems in the five countries is through the use of factor analysis of the concept data from each country. Weights were assigned to the responses of managers in each country to each of the 66 concepts as follows: four for operative values, three for intended values, two for adopted values, and one for weak values.

Analysis of the data consisted of factor analysis on the data from each country; a visual inspection of the factor structures and a comparison between countries to identify similar factors; and comparison of factor structures using the coefficient of congruence in order to provide a more conclusive index of cross-cultural factor comparisons.

The initial analysis consisted of principal factoring (Harmon, 1967) with interactions. This method assumes that only the common variance influences the patterning of variables and by removing this source the remaining correlations between variables will be zero. The procedure consists of the initial determination of the number of factors to extract from the original correlation

Table 3-11.   Average Deviation Scores for the Five Countries

	Japan	U.S.A.	Australia	India	Korea
P 25	0.57	0.64	0.65	0.70	0.77
P 50	0.83	0.92	0.96	0.96	1.01
P 75	1.11	1.24	1.26	1.23	1.26

matrix. The R^2 estimates then replace the main diagonal elements in this matrix. Next, the program uses the variances accounted for by these factors in the reduced matrix as new communality estimates. This process continues until the differences in the two successive communality estimates are negligible. The initial factors were rotated using the varimax method.

Initial inspection of the factor structures in terms of magnitudes and pattern of loadings suggested that several factors in the different countries were similar even though there were many country specific factors. Further statistical analysis seemed advisable in order to confirm or disconfirm the judgments from this visual inspection.

The final analysis of this data consisted of a paired comparison between each factor in each country with each factor in each of the other countries. The statistic used was the coefficient of congruence (Harmon, 1967). This is an index of the pattern-magnitude similarity of factor loadings. This index is like the correlation coefficient in that it ranges from −1.00 to 1.00. It differs from the correlation coefficient in not standardizing the data or equating means. This coefficient is the cosine of the angle between the factors in the space of orthoginal variables. The numerator in computing the coefficient is the sum of the cross-products of the loadings of a variable on a factor in each of the two countries being compared across all 66 concepts. The denominator is the square root of the product of the eigenvalues normalized for length prior to comparison. Coefficients of 0.75 are a minimum acceptable standard for comparison according to Harmon (1967). Coefficients of 0.85 or greater indicate considerable similarity of pattern-magnitude of the two factors compared.

The initial factor solutions yielded from 17 to 22 factors for the five countries with eigenvalues of 1.0 or greater. The final iterated solutions reduced the number of factors extracted to six to ten using this eigenvalue criterion. All the factors in the initial solutions were rotated using the varimax method. Rummell (1970) cautions against restricting the number of factors rotated in most cases because of the effect that such a procedure has on the factor structures. Subsequent discussion will emphasize only those rotated factors with significant eigenvalues in the iterated solution, however.

Tables 3-12 through 3-16 present the significant loadings (.325 or greater) for the rotated factors in each of the countries. The comparisons between the countries indicate considerable differences in terms of number of factors extracted. The United States and India solutions yielded six factors, Japan and Australia eight factors, and Korea ten factors. A visual comparison of the factors in these countries suggested that there was, however, some similarity in factors extracted in some of the countries, particularly the United States, Japan and Australia and to a lesser extent, India. The first factors in India and Australia and the sixth in Japan appeared similar to the second factor in the United States. All these factors indicate values regarding groups of employees. The third factor in Japan and the seventh in Australia seemed similar to the

Table 3-12.   Significant Rotated Factor Loadings for United States Managers

Concept	1	2	3	4	5	6
			Factors			
Trust	0.59					
Loyalty	0.55					
Dignity	0.44					
Tolerance	0.42					
Obedience	0.42					
Compassion	0.42					
Equality	0.36					
Religion	0.33					
Blue Collar Workers		0.86				
Laborers		0.69				
White Collar Employees		0.66				
Craftsman		0.57				
Technical Employees		0.56				
My Subordinates		0.40				
My Co-workers		0.33				
Organizational Effectiveness			0.47			
Organizational Growth			0.45			
Ambition			0.41			
Success			0.39			
Aggressiveness			0.38			
Profit Maximization			0.35			
High Productivity			0.33			
Owners				0.72		
Stockholders				0.72		
Change					0.57	
Risk					0.42	
Competition					0.36	
Prestige						0.61
Influence						0.59
Power						0.55

fourth United States factor. These factors indicated values concerning a group of people different from employees in their relationship to the organization, namely Owners and Stockholders. The fifth United States and seventh Japanese factors appeared similar and indicate values regarding Change, Risk and Competi-

Table 3-13. Significant Rotated Factor Loadings for Japanese Managers

Concept	Factors							
	1	*2*	*3*	*4*	*5*	*6*	*7*	*8*
Creativity	0.60							
Skill	0.57							
Ability	0.45							
Achievement	0.44							
Organizational Effectiveness	0.39							
Caution	0.38							
Profit Maximization	0.34							
Money		0.61						
Success		0.41						
Prestige		0.41						
Honor		0.35						
Stockholders			0.50					
Owners			0.50					
Labor Unions			0.43					
Obedience				0.52				
My Boss				0.43				
Leisure				0.42				
Tolerance				0.42				
Dignity					0.56			
Authority					0.38			
Power					0.34			
Influence					0.33			
Blue Collar Workers						0.73		
Craftsman						0.68		
Technical Employees						0.56		
White Collar Employees						0.39		
My Subordinates						0.37		
Managers						0.35		
Laborers						0.33		
Risk							0.68	
Change							0.61	
Competition							0.40	
Liberalism								0.52
Rational								0.48
Equality								0.39

Table 3-14.   Significant Rotated Factor Loadings for Korean Managers

Concept	Factors									
	1	2	3	4	5	6	7	8	9	10
Prejudice	0.74									
Conflict	0.74									
Conservatism	0.70									
Emotions	0.58									
Risk	0.55									
Change	0.47									
Compassion	0.40									
Leisure	0.40									
Labor Unions	0.34									
Skill		0.67								
Craftsman		0.62								
Caution		0.53								
Job Satisfaction		0.50								
Rational		0.43								
Technical Employees		0.40								
Security		0.39								
Money			0.66							
Success			0.51							
Achievement			0.33							
Managers				0.66						
Customers				0.45						
Organizational Growth				0.39						
Dignity					0.52					
Power					0.43					
Industrial Leadership					0.40					
Prestige					0.36					
My Subordinates						0.67				
Blue Collar Workers						0.53				
Organizational Stability						0.35				
High Productivity							0.73			
Organizational Stability							0.42			
Profit Maximization							0.34			
Organizational Growth							0.33			
Employee Welfare								0.62		
Social Welfare								0.57		
Employees								0.42		
Labor Unions								0.41		
Cooperation								0.40		

Table 3-14. (cont.)

	Factors									
Concept	*1*	*2*	*3*	*4*	*5*	*6*	*7*	*8*	*9*	*10*
My Co-workers									0.66	
Individuality									0.47	
My Boss									0.45	
White Collar Employees									0.35	
Tolerance									0.33	
Liberalism										0.63
Compassion										0.58
Conformity										0.55
Tolerance										0.54
Influence										0.45
Obedience										0.38
Equality										0.34
Loyalty										0.34
Honor										0.34

tion. Finally, this initial visual inspection suggested some similarity between the Indian third, Australian fourth, Japanese fifth and United States sixth factors since they indicate a power-influence set of values.

In order to confirm or refute these initial observations the factor matrixes for each of the five countries were paired with those of the remaining four. These pair comparisons were tested for similarity and differences of the value structures using the coefficient of congruence as an index. Table 3-17 presents the results of this analysis.

An examination of these results confirms some similarity of value structures of managers in the United States, Japan and Australia. These countries have similar value structures for groups of employees and owner-stockholders. In addition, Indian managers have similar value structures regarding groups of employees to those of the United States and Australia but not Japan. An examination of the pattern and magnitude of loadings for this factor in each of the countries indicates differences in both of these aspects between Japan and India on those items where overlap occurs. For the United States and Australia, differences exist only in the magnitude of loadings. Additionally, there are more items which overlap between the United States, Australia and Japan in terms of magnitude of loadings than is the case between Japan and India.

United States and Japanese managers are also similar in terms of their value structures regarding Change, Risk and Competition.

Finally, similarity exists in the value structure of United States and Australian managers regarding Power and Influence. This similarity does not occur between these countries and Japan and India. A closer examination

Table 3-15.   Significant Rotated Factor Loadings for Australian Managers

Concept	Factors							
	1	2	3	4	5	6	7	8
Blue Collar Workers	0.85							
Laborers	0.78							
White Collar Employees	0.77							
Technical Employees	0.62							
Craftsman	0.59							
My Co-workers	0.50							
My Subordinates	0.45							
Employees	0.45							
Managers	0.37							
Labor Unions	0.37							
Equality		0.58						
Social Welfare		0.54						
Tolerance		0.51						
Compassion		0.49						
Employee Welfare		0.37						
Ability			0.69					
Skill			0.63					
Success			0.39					
Aggressiveness			0.35					
Influence				0.66				
Power				0.45				
Prestige				0.38				
Autonomy					0.58			
Ambition					0.43			
Individuality					0.41			
Creativity					0.34			
Prejudice						0.63		
Force						0.47		
Conflict						0.43		
Risk						0.38		
Stockholders							0.76	
Owners							0.63	
Organizational Stability								0.51
Dignity								0.44
Organizational Effectiveness								0.40

Table 3-16. Significant Rotated Factor Loadings for Indian Managers

Concept	1	2	3	4	5	6
Blue Collar Workers	0.78					
Laborers	0.75					
White Collar Employees	0.44					
Loyalty		0.69				
Trust		0.49				
Obedience		0.43				
Money			0.52			
Power			0.48			
Force			0.37			
Property			0.35			
Influence			0.33			
Employee Welfare				0.63		
Social Welfare				0.53		
Compromise				0.36		
Rational					0.64	
Liberalism					0.33	
Industry Leadership						0.50
Competition						0.35
Organizational Growth						0.33

suggests some possible reasons for the differences in the power-influence factors of these latter countries from the former countries. The power-influence factors in Australia and the United States seem to be a general value orientation of the individual without being tied to any particular object. Additionally, these value orientations are toward personal rather than positional power and influence. The Indian power-influence factor has a more ascribed orientation to it, being tied closely to money and property and force as a mode of influence. In Japan the power-influence factor relates more closely to formal position or role and the dignity associated with that position.

One final point is worth noting regarding these value structures even where similarities do exist; namely, the differences in order of extraction of the factors. The groups of employees factor was the first factor extracted in Australia and India, the second in the United States, but the sixth in Japan. Similarly, the owners-stockholders factor is the third in Japan, fourth in the United States, but seventh in Australia. Smaller differences also exist between

Table 3-17. Coefficients of Congruence Between Rotated Factors for Pairs of Countries

Factor Name	Groups of Employees			Owners-Stockholders		Change-Risk-Competition	Power-Influence
Country \ Country	Australia Factor 1	Japan Factor 6	India Factor 1	Australia Factor 7	Japan Factor 3	Japan Factor 7	Australia Factor 4
United States Factor 2	0.94	0.86	0.86				
Australia Factor 1		0.85	0.83				
United States Factor 4				0.89	0.82		
Australia Factor 7					0.80		
United States Factor 5						0.75	
United States Factor 6							0.76

the United States and Japan on the change-risk-competition factor (five and seven respectively) and Australia and the United States on the power-influence factor (four and six respectively). Thus while the value structures are similar in pattern and magnitude they differ in terms of percentage of variance accounted for.

The direct comparison of the factors in the values systems of managers in these five countries yielded several interesting observations. First, while there is some similarity in value systems between managers in different countries there is also considerable difference. The United States was the only country in which as many as half of the factors were similar to those in other countries. Even among countries which are highly industrialized like Japan and the United States or among countries more similar in culture such as Australia and the United States, the majority of the value factors are nation-specific. A possible explanation is that cultural differences among these countries are much greater than cultural similarities, overwhelming even the similarities due to level of industrialization. This may be particularly the case in India and Korea. The similarity of the United States managers' value structures to those of managers in Japan and Australia stems, possibly, from the exportation of the culture as well as the technology of this country. The lesser degree of similarity between Japan and Australia, if this explanation is correct, would stem more from the rationale of industrialization as a force in making cultures more homogeneous.

It is interesting to note that there is no similarity between Japan and Korea. This comes somewhat as a surprise given their proximity and past political ties. If the explanation above is correct it would suggest that the cultures are, indeed, quite different and that the homogeneous influence of industrialization has not occurred in Korea where this influence is just beginning to emerge. South Korea has been a predominantly agrarian society with most of the industry in North Korea. Only recently has there been an emphasis on industrial development. The factors in Korea would seem to suggest that values more characteristic of an agrarian society and values more characteristic of an industrial culture are contemporaneous.

SUMMARY OF MANAGERIAL VALUE SIMILARITY AND DIFFERENCES IN THE FIVE COUNTRIES

The results of the analyses reported in this chapter certainly suggest that it is an oversimplification to say that the value systems in the five countries are similar or to say the opposite, that they are very different. Both similarity and difference are exhibited and we must consider both. First, it was noted that there was considerable variation in the primary orientations of managers in the five countries. The extent of pragmatic orientation was highest in Japan and lowest in India. The extent of moralistic orientation was highest in India and lowest in Korea. These differences, however, should be placed in the context of primary orientation similarity among the countries. At least 34 percent of the managers in each country were pragmatists, at least 9 percent in each country were moralists, at least 1 percent in each country were affect-oriented and at least 11 percent in each country had a mixed orientation. This suggests a primary orientation similarity for about 55 percent of the managers across all five countries.

Next, it was noted that there were significant differences in operative value scores on 29 percent of the possible country-concept pairings. This figure is much greater than the 5 percent difference that we would expect by chance if the countries were not different at all, but it is much lower than the 100 percent difference one would get if there was complete difference between the countries on each of the 66 concepts. Again, we have significant and meaningful differences but we have similarity as well.

When one correlates the operative value score on the 66 concepts for the five countries, the correlations range from .95 (U.S.A. and Australia) to .64 (Australia-Japan and Australia-Korea). The median correlation for the ten country pairs is .74. A correlation of .74 indicates that 55 percent of the variance is common between the two sets correlated. Thus, we could say, that on the average, 55 percent of the variance is common between any two pairs of countries.

Factor analysis of each country's data resulted in from six to ten factors in each country. The United States and India had the least factors while Korea had the most. About 15 percent of the possible factor comparisons from country to country had a reasonable degree of similarity. Again, we have some similarity but certainly more dissimilarity.

There are differences in the homogeneity of value systems within the five countries. Japanese managers are most similar to each other in this respect, having an average deviation score of .83 on the 66 concepts while Korean managers are most dissimilar to each other, having an average deviation score of 1.01 on the 66 concepts.

Viewing all of our results, it seems that countries are contributing from 30 to 45 percent to the variability we find while individuals are contributing from 55 to 70 percent. Thus we might say that individual differences account for about two-thirds of the variations in value systems of managers while country differences account for about one-third of the variations in value systems of managers in the five countries studied.

Chapter Four

Relationships Between
Values and Other Variables

The focus of this chapter is on the relationship between personal value systems of managers and a number of variables of interest. We are interested in how value systems of managers are related to their behavior, how value systems are related to the success of managers, how value systems are related to the job satisfaction of managers and to value differences observed when we divide our data on several organizational variables (size of organization, level of the manager in the organization and type of organization) and a personal variable (age).

We turn first to the important topic of values and behavior.

MANAGERIAL VALUES AND BEHAVIOR

The theoretical rationale presented earlier indicated that personal value systems are expected to influence both an individual's perception of problems and the decisions he makes in attempting to resolve them. In order to analyze these relationships, a behavioral measures questionnaire was developed to provide a measure of self-reported behavior of managers when confronted with typical problem situations. This behavior simulation effort was used only with managers in Australia and India, the two countries' data which was most recently collected; therefore, our results will be confined to these two countries. The questionnaire consisted of five incidents, each representing a situation which a manager may encounter in the performance of his job. The incidents were developed to cover a budgeting problem, a problem dealing with a morally questionable procedure for obtaining research and development funds, a problem dealing with the selection of an assistant and a delegation of authority problem. Managers were asked to read each incident carefully and then to indicate the action they would take by checking the appropriate statement from a list of suggested actions.

Tables 4-1 through 4-5 show the response distribution of all Indian managers and of all Australian managers to each job incident. The response distributions of the five job incidents in both countries show sufficient variability to permit relating them to the personal value systems of the managers.

While there are many ways in which one could look at the relationship between personal value systems and reported behavior of these managers, the most appropriate approach seemed to us to be that of making predictions about behavior based on rational or logical expectations generated from value responses to specific concepts in the PVQ. For example, with reference to Job Incident A, our research group developed the following rational expectations:

1. Managers who have Employee Welfare as an operative value will be willing to spend *more* money on redoing the cafeteria and rest room facilities than will managers who do not have Employee Welfare as an operative value.
2. Managers who have Profit Maximization as an operative value will be willing to spend *less* money on redoing the cafeteria and rest room facilities than will managers who do not have Profit Maximization as an operative value.
3. Managers who have Employees as an operative value will be willing to spend *more* money on redoing the cafeteria and rest room facilities than will managers who do not have Employees as an operative value.

Both the logic of the concept predictions and the use of operative values as being more behaviorally relevant than nonoperative values are thus involved in these expectations. We are actually making directional behavior predictions (spend more, spend less) for logically selected concepts for each job incident.

Table 4-6 shows the concept expectations for each job incident, the directional behavior expectation and whether or not the data supported our expectation for the Indian managers.

Two examples will show the way in which the results in Table 4-6 were generated. In Job Incident C, one of the concepts that was rationally chosen was Compassion. The reasoning was that managers for whom Compassion was an operative value would be less willing to obtain research and development funds by depriving employees of part of a potential wage increase than would managers for whom Compassion was not an operative value. The total sample of managers was thus separated into two groups; those for whom Compassion was an operative value and those for whom it was not. The response of each manager was then assigned a weight of from one to ten depending on the category of willingness that had been checked. A weight of ten was assigned to the "most willing" category and a weight of one to the "least willing" category. The mean response was then calculated for the two groups of managers with the following results:

Table 4-1. Job Incident A

Assume that you are the owner-director of a small manufacturing company. Recently, your employees have been complaining about the cafeteria and rest room facilities at the factory. These facilities were remodeled 25 years ago, and since then they have had only routine maintenance. Knowing that the anticipated profits for the year are Rs. 100,000* (about average for the company), which of the following actions would you take?

Percent Responding		
Australia	India	
10	16	— Installation of new equipment, complete repainting and cleaning—expected cost Rs. 30,000.*
65	57	— Partial installation of new equipment, complete repainting and cleaning— expected cost Rs. 12,000.*
25	26	— Major repairs, repainting and cleaning— expected cost Rs. 3,000.*
0	1	— Leave the facilities as they are.

*These values were in dollars for the Australian managers.

Managers for whom Compassion is an operative value	Managers for whom Compassion is not an operative value
N = 48	N = 403
Mean willingness score 6.14	Mean willingness score 6.62

Thus the responses are in the expected direction and the actual data is viewed as supporting the rational expectation.

For Job Incident D, one of the concepts that was rationally chosen was Cooperation. It was reasoned that managers for whom Cooperation was an operative value would choose Ram Lal more frequently than would managers for whom Cooperation was not an operative value. The actual results were as follows:

Managers for whom Cooperation is an an operative value	Managers for whom Cooperation is not an operative value
N = 286	N = 215
Percentage choosing Ram Lal = 34.3	Percentage choosing Ram Lal = 24.5

Table 4-2.   Job Incident B

Assume that you are the manager of the Research and Development Department. In your section are ten engineers who specialize in a phase of engineering in which there have been great breakthroughs in knowledge. As a result, it is only the engineers who have graduated in the last few years who are trained with respect to the new knowledge.

You, as the manager of this section, have been asked to make a recommendation about retraining the "obsolete" engineers or letting them go and hiring recent graduates. You have found that retraining would take about six months of full time study on the part of the "obsolete" engineers, and it is not certain that all would successfully complete training. You know that these ten engineers have made significant contributions to the company in the past and have an average tenure of seven years.

Which of the following would you recommend?

Percent Responding		
Australia	India	
16	15	— Retrain all the engineers and have the company pay all retraining costs.
11	7	— Retrain all the engineers and have the costs of retraining shared equally by the company and the individuals.
64	62	— Retrain only those engineers who are judged to be "trainable" and have the company pay all retraining costs.
8	8	— Retrain only those engineers who are "trainable" and have the cost of retraining shared equally by the company and the individual.
1	8	— No retraining. Retain only those engineers who can continue to make significant contributions to the company.

Again, in this example, the responses are in the expected direction and the actual data supports the rational expectation.

The same general procedure was followed in each of the 25 value-job incident behavior expectations reported in Table 4-6. A total of 20 different concepts (some were utilized for more than one job incident) from all five categories of concepts were involved in testing the relationship between values and behavior.

As can be seen from Table 4-6, the logically derived expectations relating values and behavior are found to be generally supported for four of the five incidents. For Job Incident D, only one of four predictions is supported by the data. Reexamination of the logic used in selecting the concepts and detailed examination of the data do not provide any explanation as to why expectations are so poorly supported in Job Incident D.

Across all five incidents, 19 out of 25 expectations are supported by the data. These results are both statistically ($P \cong .06$) and practically significant and attest to the relationship between managerial values and self-reported behavior for Indian managers.

Table 4-3. Job Incident C

Assume that you are the general manager of a manufacturing company. Your Research and Development (R & D) Department has been working on a project aimed at the development of an automated plant which will result in a substantial reduction in the labor costs of production. It is expected that this plant can be made operational in five years if the necessary funds are available for R & D.

The problem is securing the necessary funds for R & D. One alternative, which would represent the lowest cost to the company, is as follows: The production workers are union members. The union has been pushing for a pension plan for its members and it is willing to accept a plan in which the benefits become available only after an employee has put in 20 years of service with the company. The company has been opposed to the plan because it was felt that the potential costs of such a plan could not be accurately estimated.

Contract negotiations are coming up in a few months. In view of the projected automated plant, the company will no longer need most of the current work force after five years, and, therefore, the cost of accepting the pension plan would be relatively small. You have also ascertained that the union will accept a general wage increase of about 25 rupees* per month less than what would be the case if the pension plan is not adopted. Assume that the total number of production hours per year are such that the required funds for R & D can be obtained through reduction in production cost in this way.

Indicate your willingness to obtain the R & D funds by putting (√) at the appropriate place.

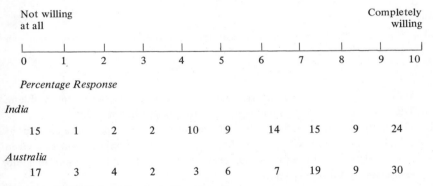

Not willing
at all

Completely
willing

| 0 | 1 | 2 | 3 | 4 | 5 | 6 | 7 | 8 | 9 | 10 |

Percentage Response

India

| 15 | 1 | 2 | 2 | 10 | 9 | 14 | 15 | 9 | 24 |

Australia

| 17 | 3 | 4 | 2 | 3 | 6 | 7 | 19 | 9 | 30 |

*Expressed in cents/hour for Australian managers.

The same procedure was followed for the Australian managers and Table 4-7 shows the concept expectations for each job incident, the directional behavior expectation, and whether or not the data supported our expectations for the Australian managers.

As seen in Table 4-7, the logically derived expectations relating values and behavior are found to be generally supported for all five incidents. Across all five incidents, 18 out of 25 expectations are supported by the data. These results attest to the relationship between managerial values and self-reported behavior for Australian managers.

The positive nature of theese results should be viewed in light of three considerations:

1. The behavior we are measuring is only simulated on the job behavior.

Table 4-4.   Job Incident D

Assume you are the administrative manager in a company and you are evaluating two senior clerks for a newly created position of assistant manager in your department. Both have worked for you for the past five years and are equally competent. However, the two men differ in the following way:

Sham Lal* is a very creative man who has been constantly making suggestions for improvement in office procedures. Although all his ideas are not practical ones, you have, in the past, adopted some of his suggestions. Sham Lal is sincere and hard working, and he can be helpful to others, if he is asked for his help. He is, however, not a very popular man in the department, because other employees do not like procedural changes and extra pressures which they think are unnecessary at times.

Ram Lal,* equally efficient as Sham Lal, is not a "man of ideas." He, on the other hand, is a very congenial and well-liked person. He goes out of his way to help others whenever they have problems. He is definitely contributing to the good morale of your department. He enjoys the reputation of a kind man.

You are chairman of a ten member committee which is considering this question. Please indicate through (√) mark:

Whom would you recommend:

	Response		*Response*	
India	Sham Lal	70%	Ram Lal	30%
Australia		75%		25%

*The names were Robin Sharp and John Roberts respectively for the Australian managers.

Managers are actually indicating how they would deal with the problem. Their actual behavior in a real work situation might be different.

2. The results are obtained even though we are considering only one concept at a time. If one were to use all of the concept expectations relevant to a given job incident at the same time, even greater differences in job incident responses would be expected.

3. The positive results are obtained even though there is great variability in the samples in terms of organizational data (kind of company, size of company, function and level in the organization) and personal data (age, education, salary). In other words, the value-behavior relationships are not obscured by all of the personal and organizational differences within the two samples of managers.

On balance, we view these results as strong support for the contention that values are related to behavior in meaningful ways for managers. The fact that the relationships exist within samples of managers from many different organizations all across India and Australia and from managers with varied organizational and personal backgrounds is clear evidence of the role of personal values in influencing problem-solving and decision-making behavior. Personal values are certainly a relevant variable in understanding the behavior of managers.

Table 4-5. Job Incident E

Assume that you are appointed as the manager of a recently organized personnel division of a middle sized manufacturing company. You have a personnel assistant in your division who directly reports to you and is of roughly similar background as yours. You are responsible for the total operation of your division. Given that you have to hire two skilled workers for the Quality Control Section of the company, which of the following functions would you delegate to your assistant?

Please note that the following functions are arranged in sequential order so that each subsequent function includes all the preceding functions.

Percent Response		
Australia	India	
0	0	— Calling employment agencies and placing orders.
2	6	— Calling newspapers for placing advertisements, and composing same (in addition to the preceding).
47	51	— Screening the applications and selecting a list of candidates to be recalled for interviews (in addition to the preceding).
30	26	— Interviewing the candidates, and after selecting two persons, sending them to the supervisor of Quality Control for final approval (in addition to the preceding).
11	4	—Negotiating with the candidates, if the first offer is not acceptable, and making the final offer (in addition to the preceding).

MANAGERIAL VALUES AND SUCCESS OF MANAGERS

In recent years considerable effort has been expended in attempts to predict managerial effectiveness by using maximum performance measures and typical behavior measures. Most of this effort has focused on tests of (1) intellectual abilities, (2) spatial and mechanical aptitudes, (3) perceptual accuracy, (4) motor abilities, and (5) personality and interest. According to Ghiselli's (1966) review, each measure shows average *r*s in the range of .25 to .30. Another area of potential importance, but receiving less emphasis, has been the notion of predicting managerial success from managers' personal values. The significance of investigating the value systems of managers has been elaborated in Chapter One. Based on this rationale, it seems reasonable to expect that personal value systems will influence not only the behavior of managers but their success as managers. Despite the apparent logic of the value-performance relationship, little empirical research has related values and performance of managers. The present analysis investigates the relationship between values of managers and their success as managers in four of our five countries (Korea is excluded because of insufficient data to measure success). The major focus of the analysis is comparative in nature and centers on answering the following questions:

Table 4-6.   Value-Behavior Relationship—Indian Managers

Concept	*Expected Behavior Direction for Operative Value Managers as Compared to Nonoperative Value Managers*	*Actual Behavior for Operative Value Managers as Compared to Nonoperative Value Managers*
Job Incident A		
Profit Maximization	Spend less	Spend less
Employee Welfare	Spend more	Spend more
Employees	Spend more	Spend more
	3 of 3 correct	
Job Incident B		
Technical Employees	Spend more on retraining	Spend less
Employee Welfare	Spend more	Spend more
Loyalty	Spend more	Spend more
Profit Maximization	Spend less	Spend less
	3 of 4 correct	
Job Incident C		
Employee Welfare	Less willing	Less willing
Blue Collar Workers	Less willing	Less willing
Labor Unions	Less willing	Less willing
Trust	Less willing	More willing
Loyalty	Less willing	Less willing
Compassion	Less willing	Less willing
Tolerance	Less willing	Less willing
Dignity	Less willing	Less willing
	7 of 8 correct	
Job Incident D		
Creativity	Sham Lal chosen more	Ram Lal chosen more
Change	Sham Lal chosen more	Ram Lal chosen more
Cooperation	Ram Lal chosen more	Ram Lal chosen more
Job Satisfaction	Ram Lal chosen more	Sham Lal chosen more
	1 of 4 correct	
Job Incident E		
My subordinates	Delegate more	Delegate more
Trust	Delegate more	Delegate less
Influence	Delegate less	Delegate less
Power	Delegate less	Delegate less
Authority	Delegate less	Delegate less
Caution	Delegate less	Delegate less
	5 of 6 correct	

Table 4-7. Value-Behavior Relationship—Australian Managers

Concept	Expected Behavior Direction for Operative Value Managers as Compared to Nonoperative Value Managers	Actual Behavior for Operative Value Managers as Compared to Nonoperative Value Managers
Job Incident A		
Profit Maximization	Spend less	Spend less
Employee Welfare	Spend more	Spend more
Employees	Spend more	Spend more
	3 of 3 correct	
Job Incident B		
Technical Employees	Spend more on retraining	Spend less
Employee Welfare	Spend more	Spend more
Loyalty	Spend more	Spend less
Profit Maximization	Spend less	Spend less
	2 of 4 correct	
Job Incident C		
Employee Welfare	Less willing	Less willing
Blue Collar Workers	Less willing	More willing
Labor Unions	Less willing	Less willing
Trust	Less willing	Less willing
Loyalty	Less willing	Less willing
Compassion	Less willing	Less willing
Tolerance	Less willing	Less willing
Dignity	Less willing	More willing
	6 of 8 correct	
Job Incident D		
Creativity	Robin Sharp chosen more	Robin Sharp chosen more
Change	Robin Sharp chosen more	Robin Sharp chosen more
Cooperation	John Roberts chosen more	John Roberts chosen more
Job Satisfaction	John Roberts chosen more	John Roberts chosen more
	4 of 4 correct	
Job Incident E		
My Subordinates	Delegate more	Delegate more
Trust	Delegate more	Delegate less
Influence	Delegate less	Delegate more
Power	Delegate less	Delegate less
Authority	Delegate less	Delegate less
Caution	Delegate less	Delegate more
	3 of 6 correct	

1. What is the nature of the relationship between managerial values and managerial success?
2. How similar or different are the relationships between values and success among managers in four different countries?
3. What are the distinguishing characteristics of value differences between successful managers and relatively less successful managers and what do these differences imply behaviorally?
4. What type of causal relationship is suggested? Are managers differentially successful because of their values or are their value systems different because they have achieved different levels of success?

Measures of Success

One major problem in dealing with this topic involves the definition and determination of success measurement. What is managerial success and how do we measure it?

Defining and measuring manager success in a study which samples widely across geographical areas, industries, organizations and type of positions is considerably restricted from that which would be possible if one were studying only managers from one organization.

It was our judgment that the heterogeneous nature of our samples dictated that we define and measure success in terms of objective data that were relatively easy to collect. Success was thus defined as managerial pay relative to age. This success criterion is a relative measure of personal success within the total sample of managers in each country and is not necessarily identical to organizational success or managerial effectiveness. It does, however, provide a cross-organizational measure which is sufficiently accurate for our purposes.

Our procedure for developing a measure of success was as follows:

1. Separate managers in each country into eight age categories—20-29, 30-34, 35-39, 40-44, 45-49, 50-54, 55-59, 60 and over.
2. Convert the distribution of income received by managers in each age category into a standard score with a mean of zero and a standard deviation of one.

Thus, a manager in any age category who received a high salary compared to others in his age category would receive a high relative success score (approaching 3.0) while a manager whose salary was low relative to others in his age group would receive a low relative success score (approaching −3.0). Each manager, then, had a personal success index between −3.0 and +3.0 depending upon his relative salary position within his age group.

While the success index is useful in relating relative success to value patterns, it does not indicate the extent of success differences in the samples in any meaningful way. Table 4-8 presents the average salary and the average salary

Table 4-8. Salary Comparisons of Most and Least Successful Managers

	U.S.A.		Australia		India		Japan	
	Yearly income (dollars)	Yearly income per year of age	Yearly income (dollars)	Yearly income per year of age	Yearly income (dollars)	Yearly income per year of age	Yearly income (dollars)	Yearly income per year of age
Most Successful Managers	41,739	902	25,838	570	18,448	259	43,103	848
Least Successful Managers	8,045	176	5,500	117	1,949	48	7,500	138
Ratio of High to Low	5.2	5.1	4.7	4.9	5.6	5.5	5.8	6.2

per year of age for the top and bottom 10 percent of managers in terms of their personal success score.

As shown in Table 4-8, the managers in the top 10 percent of our personal success index earn five to six times as much as do the managers in the bottom 10 percent of our personal success index. Likewise, when one divides salary by age for each individual, the most successful group earns five to six times as much per year of age as does the least successful group. It is clear, then, that our personal success measure represents meaningful variability of considerable magnitude. We are dealing with differences that really make a difference.

Data Analysis

A value score was prepared for each of the 66 concepts in the PVQ on the basis of the response of each manager by assigning weights as follows: four for the operative values, three for the intended values, two for adopted values and one for weak values. To determine the relationship between personal success and personal value systems for managers, each of the 66 concepts in the PVQ was examined to determine its degree of relationship with the success index by using the method of double cross-validation (Katzell, 1951). The procedure may be illustrated as follows:

1. Randomly separate the managerial sample into two equal size samples for each of the four countries.
2. Within each subsample, correlate the success score for all individuals with their value scores on each of the 66 concepts.
3. The final scoring keys for each country are developed by selecting those concepts which have the same direction of correlation in both samples and show at least a minimum correlation of .08 in one sample and at least a minimum correlation of .02 in the other sample. Using these two criteria, the product of the two probability values for the occurrence of each concept by chance alone will be less than .05.

The above steps were utilized to develop a special value key for each country which was not a function of chance differences but was stably related to personal success. The significant correlation results between the concepts measured by the PVQ and the managerial success index are reported in Table 4-9. It indicates that of the 66 possible correlations in each of the four countries, 28 in the Australian sample, 21 in the Indian sample, 12 in the Japanese sample and 22 in the United States sample were found to be statistically significant. This analysis also shows that there are nine concepts which have the same direction of correlation and have at least one significant relationship across the four countries. Since the probability of this occurring by chance is below .001, it seemed appropriate to develop a common key based on these nine concepts. After the four final scoring keys for each country and the common key for the

Table 4-9. Correlation of Concepts to Managerial Success

Concepts \ Countries	America	Australia	India	Japan
High Productivity	0	++	+	+
Industry Leadership	0	— —	0	+
Organizational Stability	— —	— —	0	+
Profit Maximization	++	++	++	0
Spcial Welfare	0	— —	— —	— —
Organizational Growth	0	++	0	0
Customers	0	++	++	0
Craftsmen	—	++	0	0
Managers	+	++	+	+
Owners	0	++	0	+
My Subordinates	++	+	+	+
Laborers	0	+	— —	0
My Company	+	++	—	0
Stockholders	0	++	0	—
Technical Employees	0	0	0	++
Me	+	++	+	—
Labor Unions	++	++	+	+
Ability	++	++	++	+
Obedience	— —	— —	— —	0
Trust	— —	— —	— —	0
Aggressiveness	+	++	++	++
Loyalty	— —	— —	— —	++
Prejudice	+	+	+	++
Compassion	0	+	—	— —
Cooperation	— —	—	0	0
Tolerance	0	—	— —	0
Conformity	— —	— —	— —	0
Honor	0	— —	0	0
Leisure	— —	— —	—	—
Dignity	— —	—	0	—
Achievement	++	+	++	0
Autonomy	—	++	+	—
Individuality	0	0	++	0
Influence	++	— —	0	+
Security	— —	— —	— —	—
Power	++	0	+	0
Creativity	+	+	++	0
Success	++	+	+	0
Authority	0	— —	+	+
Caution	— —	0	0	0

Table 4-9. (cont.)

Concepts \ Countries	America	Australia	India	Japan
Change	++	+	+	0
Competition	0	+	++	++
Compromise	0	– –	– –	0
Conflict	0	0	++	++
Equality	– –	–	– –	– –
Property	0	0	+	– –
Religion	– –	– –	– –	0
Risk	++	–	0	++

Note: ++ indicates a significant positive correlation.
      – – indicates a significant negative correlation.
      + indicates a positive correlation.
      – indicates a negative correlation.
      0 indicates no correlation.

four countries had been developed, the correlations between the composite value scores of each key and the success index were obtained to indicate the accuracy of the composite value scores of each key for predicting a manager's status on the success index.

Results and Discussion

Table 4-10 presents the overall correlations between the success score and the composite score of each value key for the managers in the different countries and the total sample. The correlation coefficients in Table 4-10 were obtained by correlating the success index with their five value scores (as derived from American, Australian, Indian, Japanese and the common value keys, respectively) for the American, Australian, Indian, Japanese and total sample. There are three primary results to be noted. First, tailor-made value keys developed for each country manifest the best results. As shown in Table 4-10, the relationships between personal values and personal success are .32 for American managers, .47 for Australian managers, .35 for Indian managers and .26 for Japanese managers. These relationships are all statistically significant and are of similar magnitude to the validity coefficients generally reported for predicting manager success by other types of predictors. We view these relationships as solid evidence that value patterns and success are related. Second, Table 4-10 indicates that when the special value key developed on one country is applied to another country, the validity coefficient shrinks, in some cases to nonsignificant values. This finding implies the danger of applying a validated instrument from one group to another. Third, as shown in the last row of Table 4-10, the common value key yields significant, yet moderate relation-

Table 4-10. Correlation between Value Scores and the Success Index for Managers in Four Countries

		U.S.A.	*Australia*	*India*	*Japan*	*Total Sample*
	Number of Managers[1]	878	301	500	312	1991
Number of Concepts						
Special Key Based on U.S.A. Sample	22*	.32**	.30**	.23**	.04	.27**
Special Key Based on Australian Sample	28*	.18**	.47**	.26**	.002	.23**
Special Key Based on Indian Sample	21*	.19**	.29**	.35**	0.03	0.23**
Special Key Based on Japanese Sample	12*	.05	.17**	.19**	.26**	.13**
Common Key Among the Four Countries	9*	.23**	.31**	.23**	.25**	.24**

*Concepts in each key are selected by double cross-validation.
**$p < .01$
[1] These sample sizes are slightly smaller than those reported earlier because data for computing the Success Index was missing for a few individuals.

ships across the four countries. This indicates that there may be some common elements underlying the relationship between value patterns and success across the different countries.

Since personal value systems of managers are relatively stable and do not change rapidly (Lusk and Oliver, 1972), and since values are related to success, we have explored the possibility of using values as a selection or promotion device in attempting to select individuals who will turn out to be successful. We developed expectancy tables showing the chances out of 100 of a manager with a given value score being among the top half of managers in terms of the personal success index as shown in Table 4-11. An American manager (for example) who has a value score of eleven or above would have a 75 percent chance of being included among the top half of managers in terms of success. The expectancy of inclusion decreases to 60, 46, 39 and 25 percent for decreasing levels of value scores.

Table 4-11.   Value Scores and Success Expectancy

PVQ *Value Scores*	*Number Scoring in this Range*	*Chances in 100 of Being in Top Half on Success Index (percent)*
U.S. Managers:		
11 and above	158	75
4 - 10	271	60
−3 - 3	233	46
−10 - −4	161	39
−11 and below	55	25
Australian Managers		
20 and above	15	93
15 - 19	28	75
10 - 14	44	66
0 - 9	134	48
−9 - −1	64	28
−10 and below	16	12
Indian Managers:		
10 and above	25	80
5 - 9	58	72
−4 - 4	209	52
−9 - −5	136	38
−10 and below	72	26
Japanese Managers:		
16 and above	15	67
14 - 15	36	58
8 - 13	194	36
6 - 7	39	28
5 and below	28	14

From Tables 4-10 and 4-11, it is evident that value patterns predict success and could be used in making selection and placement decisions. However, controversy due to logical, ethical and legal issues may arise. Persuasive arguments can be made that organizational vitality and adaptation to changing social and technological conditions may come about in large part because of the value mix in an organization. Selecting managers with similar value profiles might result in a static organization. While the full consequences of an individual organization having managers with similar value profiles is not known, it should be noted that the median number of concepts in the four value keys is 21.5 which represents only one-third of the total 66 concepts. Use of these value keys in selection and placement would still allow managerial values to differ in the remaining two-thirds of the concepts.

A second set of questions about the use of the PVQ in selection and placement decisions are ethical and legal in nature and center on "fair use" of such an instrument. Table 4-10 shows that when the special value keys developed from American, Australian and Indian samples are applied to the Japanese sample and when the Japanese value key is applied to the American sample, the validity coefficients shrink to nonsignificant values. These results are not surprising, however, since subjects from different cultural backgrounds have different value systems which in turn will result in differential perceptions of managerial success and performance. Although the results indicate that personal value systems do relate to managerial success, they do not show equal validity for managers from different countries.

Other researchers (Sikula, 1971; Kashefi-Zihajh, 1970; and Brunson, 1970) have shown that effective and ineffective employees within various organizations have differing values and value systems. Our study also indicates that managerial values have important and similar influences on success under different cultural conditions. Managers from the four different countries are rather similar in terms of the relationship between personal values and success. While the nature of these similarities will be considered in the following section, the reader is asked to note from Table 4-9 that a common value key which is valid across the four different countries can be developed. It seems likely, therefore, that one could develop a special value key which is valid for different subgroups within a particular population. Since the tailor-made value keys developed for specific countries manifest the best results, we believe different value keys and different expectancy tables should be developed for different subgroups and/or different organizations to promote fairness in employment decisions. Value data also must be integrated with other sources and types of data in order to obtain the optimal utilization of human resources.

The Nature of Value Differences between More and Less Successful Managers

Examination of the content of the concepts which are related to success provides additional meaning to the general questions about relationships between values and success.

Looking at the four countries comparatively, one notes that managers from the four countries are rather similar in terms of the relationship between personal values and success. The general pattern in Table 4-9 indicates that more successful managers have values seated in High Productivity, Profit Maximization, Managers, My Subordinates, Labor Unions, Ability, Aggressiveness, Prejudice, Achievement, Creativity, Success, Change, Competition and Liberalism. Less successful managers have values which emphasize Social Welfare, Obedience, Trust, Conformity, Leisure, Dignity, Security, Conservatism, Equality and Religion. Successful managers tend to emphasize pragmatic, dynamic, achievement-oriented values while less successful managers prefer more static and passive values, the latter forming a framework descriptive of organizational stasis rather than organizational and environmental flux. More successful managers favor an achievement orientation and prefer an active role in interaction with other individuals useful in achieving the managers' organizational goals. They value a dynamic environment and are willing to take risks to achieve organizationally valued goals. Relatively less successful managers have values associated with a static, protected environment in which they take relatively passive roles and often enjoy extended seniority and security in their organizational positions.

In terms of the significant differences that exist among the four countries across the 66 concepts, the most obvious one is that the relationships between the success indexes and the concept Loyalty are significantly positive for the Japanese managers but significantly negative for the managers from the other three countries. Another difference shown in Table 4-9 is that the concept Me is negatively related to the success index for the Japanese managers but is positively associated with success indexes for the American, Australian and Indian managers. The behavioral patterns and customs of the Japanese people have been deeply influenced by Confucianism which stresses a rigid relationship within a hierarchically arranged collective society. Members of each collective are expected to maintain absolute loyalty and obedience to authority in the fulfillment of their obligations. In view of this cultural background, it is not surprising that more successful Japanese managers place relatively greater emphasis upon Loyalty and relatively less emphasis upon Me than do managers in the other three countries.

Although significant correlations between values and success have been found, it seems important to ask whether these correlations represent a superficial and faulty association or an intrinsic relationship. A systematic comparison between the results of our analysis and other findings in the literature provides evidence of the intrinsic validity of the PVQ for predicting managerial success. A cluster of concepts including High Productivity, Profit Maximization, Ability, Achievement and Success might first be considered. The positive correlations between these concepts and success imply that an achievement and success motive in the direction of corporate goals is associated with increasing managerial success. Patton (1965) citing his own research and surveys by others noted the relationship between pay and profitability. It might, therefore, be expected that increasing success (as measured in the present study) would be associated with values emphasizing high productivity and a profit maximization. Bray, Grant and Katkovsky (1967) similarly cite the substantial correlation of Career Orientation and Achievement Motivation with managerial salary progress (salary corrected by initial starting salary). McClelland (1953, 1961) also points out that entrepreneurs are primarily driven by the achievement motive. They are interested in productivity, profits and success because it serves as a measure of their competence. McClelland suggests that achievement motivation precedes individual success and economic growth. Jurgensen (1966) includes productive, intelligent and enterprising in his list of characteristics most descriptive of successful key executives. The importance of ability is implicit in Williams' (1956) statement that critical executive behaviors include utilization of knowledge and services of subordinates, understanding the capabilities and limitations of his associates, and a major behavioral category concerned with technical competence. Executives are also willing, according to Williams, to work long hours to achieve their assigned objectives (work or achievement primacy rather than a leisure orientation).

A second cluster of values from the present study which are consistent with other findings include Change, Aggressiveness, Creativity, Competition, Liberalism, Social Welfare, Obedience, Trust, Conformity, Leisure, Dignity, Equality, Conservatism and Religion. More successful managers' values suggest that Change, Aggressiveness, Creativity, Competition and Liberalism are behaviorally relevant while Social Welfare, Obedience, Trust, Conformity, Leisure, Dignity, Equality, Conservatism and Religion are less behaviorally relevant. The implication of more successful managers' favoring a dynamic, relatively competitive and initiative-oriented environment versus less successful managers' orientation toward a more secure, stable and convergent environment finds considerable support in the literature. For example, Campbell et al., (1970) include competitive, creative, dedicated, energetic in their list of personal qualities said to be necessary for managerial effectiveness. Jurgensen (1966) also cites aggressive, selfstarting, determined, energetic, creative as most descriptive of successful executives and cites amiable, conforming, reserved, agreeable, conservative, kindly, mannerly, neat, cheerful, formal, courteous and modest as least descriptive of successful executives. The previously cited association of achievement motivation with managerial success also is relevant, as are the considerable number of studies noting the direct relationship of dominance and the inverse relation of dependency to managerial success (Bray, Grant and Katkovsky, 1967; Bray and Grant, 1966; Wollowich and MacNamara, 1969; and Hinrichs, 1967). Other sources also support the relationships found between the cluster of variables noted above and managerial success (Mitchell and Porter, 1967; Porter and Ghiselli, 1957; Laurent, 1962, 1970; Mahoney et al., 1961; and Dicken and Black, 1965).

A final cluster of concepts encompasses several related to groups of people including Managers, My Subordinates and Labor Unions. Managers' perceived behavioral relevance of these concepts increases with their actual success. These concepts are similar to some of those investigated by Rowland (1960), and the results obtained are consistent with the achievement orientation of successful managers noted above, the group-oriented characteristic of successful managers cited by Campbell et al. (1970), Williams' (1956) dimension of "Relations with Associates," Mahoney's (1966) "Performance-Support-Utilization," and Dicken and Black's (1965) "Ability to Cooperate."

We think the systematic comparisons described above suffice to show that the correlation between values and success is not a superficial association of nonessential characteristics. There is a real and intrinsic relationship between the level of success achieved by managers and their personal values. The nature of our study (concurrent validation strategy) does not allow any clear interpretation of the causal linkage between values and success. We do not know whether values influence success or whether success influences or changes values among managers. However, if we accept the Rokeach (1968) assumption that values have strong motivational components as well as cognitive, affective and behavioral components, it would seem that managers are differentially successful because of their values. The fact that we derived our success measure for each age group and then aggregated for all age categories argues against there being any strong cumulative effect of long-term successful experience in the relationship between success and values which we found. Our success measure is not correlated with age and total number of years that a manager has worked. The value keys we developed are minimally related to age in the four countries (*r*s ranging from −.05 to −.17).

Summary

This present analysis examines the nature of the relationship between the personal values of managers and their success as managers for samples of American, Australian, Indian and Japanese managers. While additional and extended study and analysis of managers in other countries undoubtedly will clarify the functional relationship between values and success, our evidence suggests the following general findings and conclusions.

1. There is a reasonably strong relationship between the level of success achieved by managers and their personal values. The magnitude of the relationships are indicated by the significant correlation coefficients of .32 for American managers, .47 for Australian managers, .35 for Indian managers and .26 for Japanese managers. We view these correlations as real and intrinsic relationships rather than superficial and faulty associations.

2. It is evident that value patterns are predictive of managerial success and could be used in selection and placement decisions. A number of legal and ethical issues must be considered, however, before such use is justified.

3. Although there are country differences in the relationships between values and success, the findings across the four countries are quite similar.

4. The general pattern emerging from the study indicates that more successful managers appear to favor pragmatic, dynamic, achievement-oriented values while less successful managers prefer more static and passive values, the latter forming a framework descriptive of organizational stasis rather than organizational and environmental flux. More successful managers favor an achievement orientation and prefer an active role in interaction with other individuals instrumental to achievement of the managers organizational goals.

Less successful managers have values associated with a static and protected environment in which they take relatively passive roles.

MANAGERIAL VALUES AND JOB
SATISFACTION OF MANAGERS

Each manager in the five countries responded to four items concerning his job satisfaction. These items are drawn from the Hoppock Job Satisfaction Scale and have been used extensively in job satisfaction research. The four items are shown below:

A. Choose the ONE of the following statements which best tells how well you like your job. Place a check mark in front of that statement.

      1. I hate it.
      2. I dislike it.
      3. I don't like it.
      4. I am indifferent to it.
      5. I like it.
      6. I am enthusiastic about it.
      7. I love.

B. Check one of the following to show HOW MUCH OF THE TIME you feel satisfied with your job:

      1. All the time.
      2. Most of the time.
      3. A good deal of the time.
      4. About half of the time.
      5. Occasionally.
      6. Seldom.
      7. Never

C. Check the ONE of the following which best tells how you feel about changing your job:

      1. I would quit this job at once if I could get anything else to do.
      2. I would take almost any other job in which I could earn as much as I am earning now.
      3. I would like to change both my job and my occupation.
      4. I would like to exchange my present job for another job.
      5. I am not eager to change my job, but I would do so if I could get a better job.

_____ 6. I cannot think of any jobs for which I would exchange.

_____ 7. I would not exchange my job for any other.

D. Check one of the following to show how you think you compare with other people.

_____ 1. No one likes his job better than I like mine.

_____ 2. I like my job much better than most people like theirs.

_____ 3. I like my job better than most people like theirs.

_____ 4. I like my job about as well as most people like theirs.

_____ 5. I dislike my job more than most people dislike theirs.

_____ 6. I dislike my job much more than most people dislike theirs.

_____ 7. No one dislikes his job more than I dislike mine.

These four job satisfaction items were scored by giving a weight of one to the least favorable response on each item, a two to the next least favorable response and so on up to a weight of seven for the most favorable response to each item. Any manager, then, could have a job satisfaction score ranging from four (least satisfied) to 28 (most satisfied).

The overall level of job satisfaction among the managers in the five countries is quite high as shown in Table 4-12. It is certainly not unexpected that relatively high level and highly paid managers should indicate a considerable degree of job satisfaction. Table 4-12 shows that U.S. managers have significantly greater job satisfaction; Japanese, Australian and Indian managers have equivalent levels of job satisfaction; while Korean managers have significantly lower job satisfaction. While the U.S. and Korean deviations from the other three countries are statistically significant, in a practical sense the differences are rather small.

To analyze the relationship between managerial values and job satisfaction of managers, the same procedures were used as described in the previous section of this chapter. The only difference is that here we are relating job satisfaction scores rather than a success score to managerial values. These

Table 4-12. Job Satisfaction Scores (Means and Standard Deviations) for Managers from the Five Countries

Country	Mean Satisfaction Score	Standard Deviation
U.S.	22.65	2.53
India	21.81	2.88
Japan	21.48	3.17
Australia	21.15	2.85
Korea	19.98	3.60

procedures were utilized to develop a special value key for each country which was not a function of chance differences but was stably related to managerial job satisfaction. The significant correlation results between the concepts measured by the PVQ and the job satisfaction scores are reported in Table 4-13. It shows that of the 66 possible correlations in each of the five countries, 23 in the U.S. sample, 16 in the Australian sample, 30 in the Indian sample, 26 in the Japanese sample and 31 in the Korean sample were found to be statistically significant. This analysis also shows that there are nine concepts which have the same direction of correlation for at least four of the five countries and no opposite direction correlations. Since the probability of this occurring by chance is very small, it seemed appropriate to develop a common key based on these nine concepts. After the five final scoring keys for each country and the common key for the five countries had been developed, the correlations between the composite value scores of each key and the job satisfaction scores were obtained.

Results and Discussion

Table 4-14 presents the overall correlations between the satisfaction score and the composite score of each value key for managers in the different countries and the total sample. Again, three primary results can be noted. First, tailor-made value keys developed for each country manifest the best results. As shown in Table 4-14, the relationships between personal values and job satisfaction are .24 for U.S. managers, .38 for Australian managers, .26 for Indian managers, .30 for Japanese managers and .28 for Korean managers. These relationships are all statistically significant and indicate a moderate relationship between values and job satisfaction. Second, Table 4-14 indicates that when the special value key developed on one country is applied to another country, the correlation coefficient shrinks, in many cases to nonsignificant values. Third, as shown in the last line of Table 4-14, the common key yields significant and moderate relationships between values and job satisfaction across the five countries. This indicates that there may be some common elements underlying the value-job satisfaction relationship across the countries.

The nine concepts which are commonly related to job satisfaction across the five countries (those in the common key) are Industry Leadership, Organizational Efficiency, Organizational Growth, Employee Welfare, Owners, My Company, Loyalty, Job Satisfaction and Competition. All these concepts are positively related to job satisfaction scores; thus the more behaviorally relevant the concept is, the higher the level of job satisfaction. The content of these concepts suggests that high job satisfaction is associated with a high level of affective identification with the organization. Valuing your company and its owners; valuing your company as an industry leader; being loyal and satisfied; valuing your organization's growth, efficiency and the way it treats its employ-ees—all these seem to point to high affective identification with your company.

It is interesting to note that this set of concepts which is related to

Table 4-13. Correlation of Concepts to Managerial Job Satisfaction

Concepts \ Countries	U.S.A.	Australia	India	Japan	Korea
High Productivity	0	0	++	0	++
Industry Leadership	++	++	++	+	++
Employee Welfare	+	0	++	++	++
Organizational Stability	+	+	+	++	−
Profit Maximization	++	++	0	++	0
Organizational Efficiency	++	+	+	++	+
Social Welfare	0	0	++	++	++
Organizational Growth	++	+	++	++	++
Employees	++	0	++	−	0
Customers	0	0	++	++	−
My Co-workers	++	0	0	+	0
Craftsmen	+	0	++	0	0
My Boss	++	−	++	0	++
Managers	++	0	++	++	0
Owners	++	++	++	+	0
My Subordinates	+	0	−	++	++
Laborers	0	0	+	++	++
My Company	++	++	++	+	++
Blue Collar Workers	++	0	0	+	0
Stockholders	++	0	++	0	+
Technical Employees	+	0	++	0	++
Labor Unions	0	0	++	0	++
White Collar Employees	++	0	++	0	0
Ambition	++	0	++	0	0
Ability	+	+	++	++	−
Obedience	0	−−	++	0	0
Trust	+	−−	0	0	0
Aggressiveness	++	0	0	0	++
Loyalty	++	++	+	++	++
Prejudice	0	−−	0	−	++
Compassion	−	0	0	−−	0
Skill	+	−	++	++	++
Tolerance	+	0	++	0	−−
Conformity	0	0	++	0	+
Honor	++	−	0	0	++
Leisure	0	−−	−	0	0
Dignity	0	+	++	0	0
Achievement	++	0	++	++	0

Table 4-13. (cont.)

Concepts \ Countries	U.S.A.	Australia	India	Japan	Korea
Autonomy	+	0	+	++	0
Money	0	--	0	0	--
Individuality	0	0	++	++	0
Job Satisfaction	++	0	+	++	++
Influence	++	0	0	0	+
Security	0	--	0	+	++
Power	0	0	0	-	++
Success	++	0	0	0	0
Prestige	0	0	+	++	++
Authority	++	-	0	0	++
Caution	0	0	++	++	0
Competition	+	+	++	++	++
Compromise	0	-	++	0	++
Conflict	0	--	0	--	++
Conservatism	0	0	+	--	++
Emotions	-	0	0	-	++
Equality	0	++	+	-	+
Force	+	0	0	++	0
Government	+	--	+	0	++
Liberalism	+	0	++	+	0
Rationale	+	--	++	++	0
Religion	+	-	0	0	++
Risk	††	-	+	++	++

Note: ++ indicates a significant positive correlation.
 -- indicates a significant negative correlation
 + indicates a positive correlation.
 - indicates a negative correlation.
 0 indicates no correlation.

job satisfaction is almost totally different from the set of concepts that was related to managerial success. Thus a different set of values goes with success than goes with job satisfaction. This last observation is further supported by the finding that there is negligible difference in the average Hoppock Job Satisfaction scores between the top and bottom halves of managers on our success index (job satisfaction scores of 21.1 and 21.6 respectively on the international sample).

In summary, we find that managerial values are moderately related to the level of managerial job satisfaction. While there are country differences in these relationships, the findings across the five countries are reasonably similar.

Table 4-14.   Correlation between Value Scores and Job Satisfaction for Managers in Five Countries

	Number of Concepts	Number of Managers	U.S.A.	Australia	India	Japan	Korea	Total Sample
			878	301	500	312	166	2157
Special Key Based on U.S.A. Sample	23*		.24**	.02	.18**	.16**	.11	.23**
Special Key Based on Australian Sample	16*		.09	.38**	.06	.03	.05	.17**
Special Key Based on Indian Sample	30*		.15**	.01	.26**	.15**	.10	.17**
Special Key Based on Japanese Sample	26*		.17**	.04	.18**	.30**	.11	.16
Special Key Based on Korean Sample	31*		.15**	−.02	.19**	.16**	.28**	.18**
Common Key Among the Samples of the Five Countries	9*		.21**	.15**	.23**	.21**	.20**	.25**

*Concepts in each key are selected by double cross-validation.
**$p < .01$

Across the five countries, job satisfaction tends to go with high affective identification with one's own company. U.S.A. managers are slightly more satisfied and Korean managers are slightly less satisfied than are the managers in the other three countries.

MANAGERIAL VALUES AND ORGANIZATIONAL VARIABLES

Here we are concerned with whether or not managers in large organizations have different values than do managers in small organizations; are the values of high level managers different from those of lower level managers; and do the values of managers employed in the manufacturing industry differ from those employed in nonmanufacturing companies? The procedure followed was to separate managers in each country and in the international sample into three size groups (large, medium and small), into three organizational level groups (top management, upper middle management, lower middle management) and into two industry groups (manufacturing as opposed to nonmanufacturing), and then to compare value systems of managers among the size categories, the level categories and the industry categories.

Primary Orientation and Organizational Variables

Table 4-15 shows the relationships found between primary orientation of managers and the three organizational variables. As shown in Table 4-15, the relationships are largely country-specific and do not provide any clear international picture. U.S.A., Japanese and Korean managers employed in larger size organizations are more pragmatic than those employed in smaller firms; in Australia the reverse is true, while there is no relationship between size and primary orientation in India.

Australian and Korean managers in higher level jobs are more pragmatic and less moralistic while the reverse is true for Japanese and Indian

Table 4-15. Primary Orientation and Organizational Variables

Country	Size and Primary Orientation	Organizational Level and Primary Orientation	Industry and Primary Orientation
U.S.A.	Pragmatism$^+$	No relationship	No relationship
Japan	Pragmatism$^+$	Pragmatism$^-$ Moralism$^+$	No relationship
Korea	Pragmatism$^+$	Pragmatism$^+$ Moralism$^-$	Pragmatism higher in manufacturing
Australia	Pragmatism$^-$ Moralism$^+$	Pragmatism$^+$ Moralism$^-$	No relationship
India	No relationship	Pragmatism$^-$ Moralism$^+$	No relationship
International Sample	No relationship	No relationship	No relationship

Note: $^+$indicates a positive relationship between the listed primary orientation and the organizational variable and $^-$ indicates a negative relationship.

managers. There is no relationship between primary orientation and organizational level of the manager in the United States.

Korean managers employed in manufacturing companies are more pragmatic than those employed in nonmanufacturing companies. There is no relationship between primary orientation and industry classification in the other four countries.

In summary, there are relationships between primary orientation and the organizational variables (size and level) and little relationship between primary orientation and type of industry. The primary orientation relationships found are country-specific and do not form any overall international pattern.

Value Profiles and Size
of Organization

There are differences in value profiles of managers employed in different size categories as shown in Table 4-16 but the differences are highly country-specific and do not form any overall international pattern. Size of firm seems to make the greatest difference in value patterns in Australia and the U.S.A. and the least difference in Japan.

The nature of the size differences found in each country is shown in Table 4-16 and we see little possibility of interpreting them cross-nationally.

Value Profiles and Managerial
Level

Figure 4-1 shows that internationally, higher level managers show a pattern of active and aggressive achievement of organizational goals with minimal humanistic orientation. This pattern is quite similar to that shown for more successful managers earlier in the chapter.

Value Profiles and Type
of Company

There were differences on only four of the 66 concepts between manufacturing and nonmanufacturing companies and this is about the number expected by chance. Our results, then, show no meaningful differences in value profiles for manufacturing versus nonmanufacturing companies.

MANAGERIAL VALUES AND AGE
OF THE MANAGER

There is a slight tendency for older managers to be more moralistically oriented than is the case for younger managers. This finding is consistent in all countries but Korea where the opposite is found. In the international sample, 24 percent of the young group, 26 percent of the middle age group and 29 percent of the older age group have moralistic primary orientations.

Table 4-16. Size of Firm and Operative Value Scores

	U.S.A.	Japan	Korea	Australia	India
Operative Value Scores Higher in Larger Firms	High Productivity Profit Maximization Employees My Subordinates Job Satisfaction Change	Customers Technical Employees Ability Success Competition	My Company Stockholders Individuality	My Subordinates Ability	Industry Leadership Employee Welfare Social Welfare
Operative Value Scores Higher in Smaller Firms	Organizational Stability Loyalty Cooperation Dignity Security Authority Caution Conservatism Religion	Owners	Blue Collar Workers My Subordinates Money Job Satisfaction Caution Emotions Rational	Profit Maximization Organizational Stability My Company Stockholders Customers My Co-workers My Boss Managers Owners Ambition Job Satisfaction Security Property Emotions	Tolerance Obedience Dignity Security Influence Creativity Prestige

Figure 4-1. Value Patterns and Organizational Level

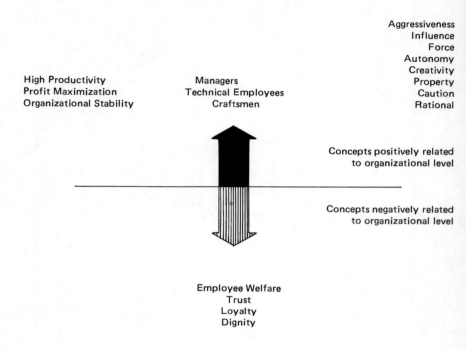

High Productivity
Profit Maximization
Organizational Stability

Managers
Technical Employees
Craftsmen

Aggressiveness
Influence
Force
Autonomy
Creativity
Property
Caution
Rational

Concepts positively related
to organizational level

Concepts negatively related
to organizational level

Employee Welfare
Trust
Loyalty
Dignity

When we look at the value profiles of managers in different age groups, there are many significant differences, but no consistent pattern emerges across the five countries. Age differences are found on 36 percent of the concepts in Japan, 26 percent in Korea, 23 percent in Australia, 15 percent in the U.S.A. and 6 percent in India. Japan, then, is the country where age makes the greatest difference in values while age seems to make little or no difference in values in India.

There is also a differential influence of age on different concept categories. For concepts dealing with groups of people and institutions, there are age differences on 33 percent of the possible concept-country combinations. The analogous percentages are 29 percent for characteristics of individuals, 18 percent for organizational goals, 12 percent for general concepts and 11 percent for personal goals.

The relationship between age and values is largely country-specific and we see little possibility of interpreting these differences cross-nationally.

Table 4-17 presents a summary of the relationships found between personal value systems of managers and the variables that have been considered in this chapter. It shows that values are significantly and cross-nationally related

Table 4-17. Summary of Relationship between Values and Other Variables

Values Related to:	Magnitude of Relationship	Cross-national Generality of Relationship
Behavior (problem solving and decision making)	Moderate 72-76 percent of predictions correct	Consistent relationships in India and Australia (only tested in these countries)
Personal success of managers	Moderate rs from .26-.47	Consistent relationships in U.S.A., Japan, Australia and India (Korea excluded from analysis)
Job satisfaction of managers	Moderate rs from .24-.38	Consistent relationships in all five countries
Organizational size (number of employees)	Moderate Differences found on 17 percent of concepts	Relationships highly country-specific
Organizational level of managers	Moderate Differences found on 27 percent of concepts	Consistent relationships in all five countries
Type of organization (manufacturing vs. nonmanufacturing)	No significant differences	No relationship in any country
Age of managers	Moderate Differences found on 21 percent of concepts	Relationships largely country-specific

to decision making and problem solving, to managerial success and to the job satisfaction of managers. Organizational level is significantly and cross-nationally related to value patterns while type of organization shows no relationship with value patterns. The value patterns of managers in different size categories and in different age groups are different but the differences are largely country specific.

Chapter Five

Personal Value Systems of Managers in Each Country

We focus our attention on each country separately in this chapter. We will bring together all that we have found about each country's managers and attempt to draw meaningful national summaries. We turn first to American managers.

AMERICAN MANAGERS

The American sample consisted of 997 managers from over 500 companies. Slightly over half of the managers were employed in manufacturing companies. Approximately one-third of the managers came from each size of company category: small—under 500 employees; medium size—500 to 4999 employees; and large organizations—5000 and over employees. The sample was relatively well spread over nine major functional areas. About one-third of the managers were in line positions, one-third in staff positions and one-third in combined line-staff positions. Fifty-seven percent of the managers were in distinctly top management level jobs (president and vice president), 31 percent were in upper level middle management (jobs reporting to the vice presidential level) and 13 percent were in lower level middle management (two to four levels below the vice presidential level). The median salary for the sample is $24,000 a year; the median number of years of managerial experience is 13; while the median age in the sample is 47 years. American managers report a very high degree of job satisfaction, being the most satisfied group among the five countries.

We classify 57 percent of these American managers as having a pragmatic orientation, 30 percent as having a moralistic orientation and only 1 percent as having an affect orientation. American managers, then, are largely pragmatic in nature and secondarily moralistic in nature. We find that the degree of pragmatism among American managers increases from small to large companies but is not related to level in the organization, type of company or to the age of the manager.

Figure 5-1 presents a value profile for the American managers which shows the behavioral relevance score for each of the 66 concepts in the PVQ and categorizes the concepts into operative values, intended values, adopted values or weak values for the total sample of American managers. It will be remembered from earlier discussion that operative values are most highly internalized into the value system of the managers and are most readily translated into behavior. Intended values are felt to be important but have not been organizationally reinforced to a large extent by the managers' experience and are less likely to be translated from intentionality into behavior. Adopted values are not viewed as important by the managers but have been reinforced in their organizational experience. Their influence on behavior is largely situation-dependent. Weak values are those that are viewed as neither important nor fitting one's experience and are expected to influence behavior minimally.

When we look at the content of the operative values for American managers from Figure 5-1, several observations can be made. Managers have internalized organizational goals to a relatively high degree and would be expected to behave in reference to them. This is particularly true of efficiency, productivity and profit. It is true to a lesser extent for growth, industry leadership, and stability. Employee Welfare is a mid-level intended value while Social Welfare is a very weak value.

American managers view a large number of employee groups with which they interact as relevant reference groups and their behavior would be expected to be shaped by these groups. This finding is much stronger for American managers than for any of the other four countries and suggests that groups of people are indeed a relevant part of the American managerial value system.

A high level of competence orientation is suggested for American managers when we see that Ability, Ambition, Skill, Cooperation and Competition are a part of their operative value set.

American managers have a high achievement orientation as shown by the personal goal concepts Achievement, Creativity, Success and Job Satisfaction being a part of their operative value set. It is notable that Security and Autonomy are very weak personal goals for these managers.

When we look at the intended values for American managers we see an intended humanistic orientation (Trust, Loyalty, Honor, Employee Welfare, Individuality, Dignity and Religion). The extent to which this intended humanistic orientation gets translated into behavior is problematical and probably depends upon the extent to which it is in agreement or in conflict with the organizational goal orientation, the competence orientation and the achievement orientation that were found in the operative value set.

The adopted value category forms a set of behavioral strategies that are defined by Aggressiveness, Change, Authority, Money, Risk and Compromise. These adopted behavioral strategies are probably used when the situation calls for them and their influence on behavior is certainly problematical. The

Figure 5-1. Value Profile—American Managers

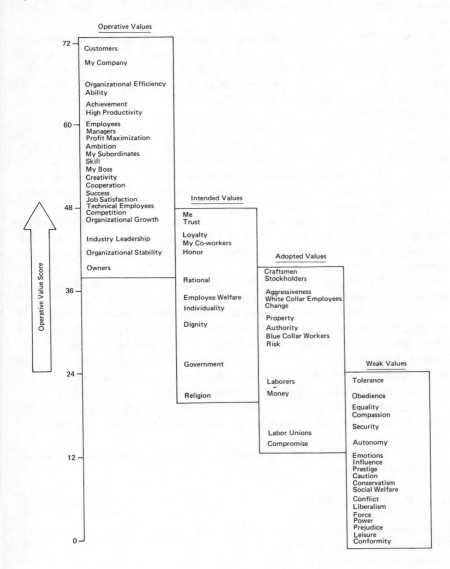

fact that American managers are pragmatic to a large extent would suggest that these adopted behavioral strategies will indeed be used when needed.

The set of weak values for American managers includes Conformity, Social Welfare, Autonomy, Security, Compassion, Equality, Obedience and Tolerance. It is suggested that managers clearly reject organizational egalitarianism as a part of their value structure. Such an egalitarian orientation would be in direct conflict with their competence and achievement orientations and it is rejected.

When we compare American managers to those from the other four countries, several additional observations can be made. The value system of American managers differs the least of any of the five countries from the international sample of managers which is comprised of a random sample of 150 managers from each of the countries. This same universalistic or modal value pattern of American managers is noted when we observe that a higher proportion of the factors (found from factor analysis) in the American sample are similar to factors in other countries. One could speculate that the U.S.A. exports not only technology but managerial values as well.

The American manager value system is the least complex of those found in any of the countries in a factorial sense; only six factors were found when the value system was factor analyzed.

The value system of American managers shows a mid-level of homogeneity (similarity of one manager to another), considerably less homogeneous than Japanese managers and more homogeneous than Indian or Korean managers.

The overall value pattern of American managers is most similar to that of Australian managers and least similar to that of Korean managers.

We also have evidence that the value system of American managers is remarkably stable over a six year time period (1966 to 1972) when there was a considerable amount of social and environmental change within the country. Singer (1973) also has reported a high level of value consistency over a ten year period for a sample of 100 top level American managers as measured by the Allport, Vernon and Lindzey *Study of Values* (1960).

American managerial value systems are related to managerial success and to job satisfaction of the manager in a way similar to that found in the other countries.

In summary, the outstanding value characteristics of American managers as a group are:

1. pragmatic orientation,
2. organizational goal orientation,
3. competence orientation,
4. relevancy of groups orientation,
5. achievement orientation,
6. intended humanistic orientation, and
7. rejection of an organizational egalitarian orientation.

AUSTRALIAN MANAGERS

The Australian sample consisted of 351 managers drawn from nearly 200 organizations. Nearly half of the managers were employed in manufacturing companies. Nearly half were also from companies with less than 250 employees, about one-third were from companies with 250-1999 employees and about one-fifth of the managers were employed in companies having 2000 or more employees. About 40 percent of the managers reported general administration as their major job function while six other functions were reasonably well represented. About a third of the managers were in line positions, 24 percent in staff positions and 42 percent in combined line-staff positions. Fifty-eight percent of the managers were in top management positions, 26 percent were in upper middle management positions, while 12 percent were in lower level middle management positions. The median salary is $13,700 (U.S. dollars) a year; the median number of years of managerial experience is 15; while the median age of the sample is 47 years. Australian managers report a high level of job satisfaction; somewhat less satisfied than American managers, about the same as Japanese and Indian managers, and somewhat more satisfied than Korean managers.

We classify 40 percent of our sample of Australian managers as pragmatists, 40 percent as moralists and 5 percent as affect-oriented. Australian managers, then, have a relatively high level of moralistic orientation (compared to other countries) and a rather low level of pragmatic orientation. The degree of moralistic orientation increases from small to large companies while the degree of pragmatism decreases. The degree of pragmatic orientation increases as level in the organization becomes higher while the degree of moralism decreases. There is no meaningful difference in primary orientation between managers employed in manufacturing and those in nonmanufacturing companies. Older Australian managers tend to have a more humanistic orientation than do younger managers although both groups are relatively high in this respect.

Figure 5-2 presents a value profile for the Australian managers which shows the behavioral relevance score for each of the 66 concepts in the PVQ and categorizes the concepts into operative values, intended values, adopted values and weak values.

Looking at the operative values for Australian managers suggests several observations. These managers have internalized the organizational goals, efficiency and productivity, to a considerable extent but have not internalized industry leadership, stability, profit and growth to a very large extent. When compared to other countries, Australian managers are extremely low on profit and growth. This implies that Australian managers have not internalized many of the goals of the organization to a marked degree and their behavior would not be highly responsive to organizational goal considerations. The goal Employee Welfare is a high level intended value for Australian managers and has greater behavioral significance for them than is the case in the other countries.

The set of concepts Skill, Ability, Cooperation, Trust, Loyalty, Achievement, Job Satisfaction, Honor and Ambition suggests a competence orientation that is humanistic in nature as opposed to being personal or organizational in focus. The fact that eight groups of people are among the operative set of values further reinforces the notion of a humanistic orientation for Australian managers.

Figure 5-2.   Value Profile—Australian Managers

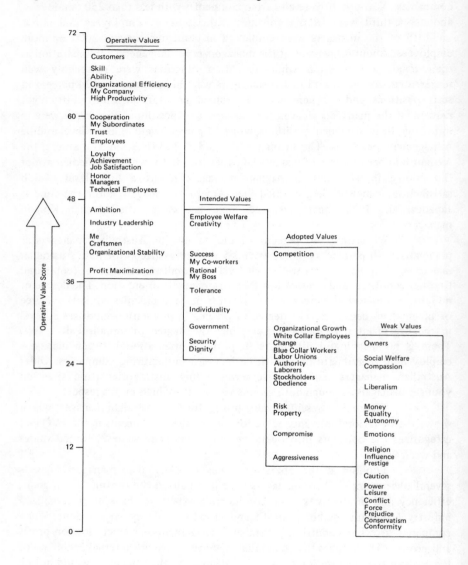

The fact that Creativity and Success are intended values while Competition, Change, Risk and Aggressiveness are adopted values for Australian managers suggests a much lower level of achievement orientation than was found for American managers. Personal and organizational achievement is thus problematical for Australian managers and its operation in behavior would seem to depend upon whether or not it was consistent with the overriding humanistic orientation of these managers.

The set of weak values for Australian managers is very similar to those found for the American sample but we are less certain that Australian managers do in fact reject organizational egalitarianism as a part of their value structure as did American managers. The relatively high behavioral relevance scores (compared to other countries) for Australian managers on Tolerance, Compassion, Trust, Loyalty, Honor, Employee Welfare and Social Welfare would seem likely to temper this rejection of egalitarianism. At the very least, Australian managers do not reject egalitarianism to the same extent that American managers do.

The Australian manager value system is at a mid-level of complexity in a factorial sense with eight factors emerging when the value system was factor analyzed.

The value system of Australian managers shows a mid-level of homogeneity (similarity of one manager to another), considerably less homogeneous than Japanese managers and more homogeneous than Indian or Korean managers.

The overall value pattern of Australian managers is most similar to that of American managers and least similar to that of Japanese and Korean managers.

Although detailed data are not shown, there is considerable geographical variation in the value system of Australian managers. Managers from Western Australia and Tasmania are the two most different states in this respect.

Australian managerial value systems are related to management success and to job satisfaction of the manager in a way similar to that found in the other countries. Managerial behavior (decision making and problem solving) is related to value patterns of managers to a considerable extent and in a similar manner as found for Indian managers.

In summary, the outstanding value characteristics of Australian managers as a group are:

moralistic orientation,
high level humanistic orientation,
low organizational goal orientation,
low level personal and organizational competence orientation, and
relatively low level of achievement orientation.

INDIAN MANAGERS

The Indian sample consisted of 623 managers from private enterprise organizations in India. About 60 percent of the managers were employed in manufacturing companies. Approximately one-third of the managers came from each size of company category: small—under 250 employees; medium—250 to 999 employees; large—1000 and over employees. Nearly half of the managers reported general administration as their job function and there was reasonable representation in five other job functions. Twenty-one percent were in line positions while 31 percent and 48 percent were in staff and combined line-staff positions, respectively. Forty-seven percent were in top management positions, 43 percent in upper middle management and 10 percent in lower middle management positions. The median salary was $4300 per year. The median years of managerial experience was 11, while the median age was 43 years. Indian managers have a high level of job satisfaction; somewhat lower than that reported by American managers but somewhat higher than Korean managers.

We classify 44 percent of Indian managers as having a moralistic orientation, 34 percent as having a pragmatic orientation and only 2 percent as having an affective orientation. Indian managers then are largely moralistic in nature and secondarily pragmatic. The degree of moralistic orientation increases and pragmatism decreases with increased organizational level and with age of managers. There is no relationship between primary orientation and size or type of company for Indian managers.

Figure 5-3 presents a value profile for the Indian managers. With respect to organizational goal concepts, three subsets are formed. The operative value subset includes the goals Organizational Efficiency, High Productivity and Organizational Stability. For Indian managers, these seem to be what Simon (1964) calls maximization criteria. They (efficiency, productivity and stability) are the goals which managers attempt to influence directly by their actions, decisions and behavior and are useful in generating alternative courses of action or ways of behaving.

A second subset of organizational goals are intended and adopted values and consist of Organizational Growth, Employee Welfare, Industry Leadership and Profit Maximization. The secondary position of these goals in terms of behavioral relevance and value type would suggest that they be viewed as desirable and intended goals. They may not be sought in and of themselves; rather they may be used as constraints in alternative testing. Managers may decide on given actions to influence the "maximization criteria" goals and then infer or check the expected impact of these actions on the goals in this second subset.

The final subset of organizational goals includes only Social Welfare which is viewed as an operative value by only 18 percent of the managers while 52 percent view it as a weak value. Therefore, it would be expected to have relatively little impact on behavior.

Concepts dealing with personal goals of individuals form an important part of the value system of Indian managers. Job Satisfaction, Achievement, Creativity, Success, Prestige and Individuality are the personal goals that represent operative values for managers. Dignity and Security represent intended values for managers. It is suggested that these two sets of concepts are keystones in the motivational structure underlying Indian managerial behavior. These

Figure 5-3. Value Profile—Indian Managers

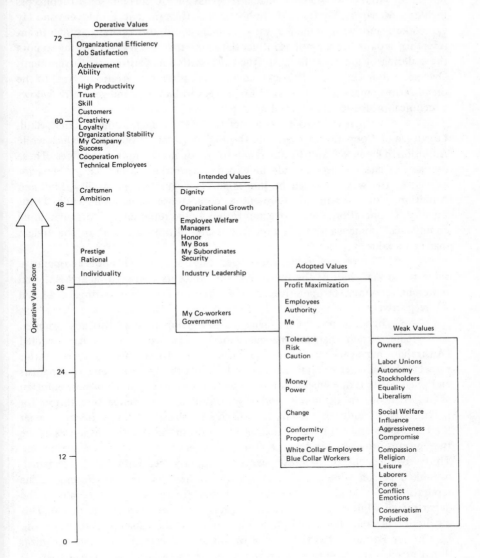

concepts represent the personal goals that managers are striving to attain and their relatively high level of operative value scores suggests that a high degree of "personalism" is involved in the Indian manager value system.

With respect to groups of people and institutions, the set of concepts including Customers, My Company, Technical Employees and Craftsmen represent the highest level of operative values for managers and are used as significant reference groups in shaping manager behavior. A second set of concepts including Managers, My Boss, My Subordinates, Government, Employees and My Co-workers represent intended values which could also operate as significant reference groups but are not as influential as the first set. It is interesting to note the ordering of groups external to the organization as Customers, Government, Owners, Labor Unions and Stockholders. The ordering of groups internal to the organization ranges from Technical Employees to Laborers and generally follows a technical-professional-skill level hierarchy.

With respect to ideas associated with people, Ability, Trust, Skill, Loyalty and Cooperation represent the highest level of operative values while Ambition, Obedience and Honor represent moderately important values. These two sets of characteristics would be expected to influence a manager's behavior as well as the way in which he judges and evaluates others. Ability, Skill and Ambition would seem to represent a competence dimension while Trust, Loyalty, Cooperation, Obedience and Honor would represent an "organizational compliance" dimension. Both dimensions are obviously a part of the Indian manager's value system.

With respect to ideas about general topics, no concept is an operative value for at least half of the managers. The concepts Competition and Rational represent second level operative values for the managers with scores of 44 and 40, respectively.

In summary, Indian managers as a group are moralistically oriented to a greater extent than are managers in the other countries we have studied (Australian managers, however, are rather close to Indian managers in this respect). In India, the major distinction between the value systems of moralists and pragmatists is one where moralists have a bureaucratic humanism orientation as opposed to an economic and organizational competence orientation for pragmatists. In addition, pragmatic managers are slightly younger, occupy higher level positions and earn higher incomes than do moralists. The responses of the two groups on Job Incident D also lend support to the above distinction. Thirty-five percent of moralist managers would select Ram Lal (a congenial, well-liked person who goes out of his way to help others and who enjoys the reputation of a kind man and one who contributes to good morale in the department) while only 25 percent of pragmatists would select Ram Lal. This distinction in values between moralists and pragmatists is analogous to that made by Chester Barnard (1938) between organizational effectiveness and organizational efficiency. Barnard saw organizational effectiveness as a measure of the extent to which an organization achieved its goals while organizational efficiency was viewed as a combination measure of the extent to which it achieved its goals and satisfied the needs of its members. Pragmatists' value systems are more in line with the notion of organizational effectiveness while moralists' value systems are more in accord with the notion of organizational efficiency.

Indian managers as a group place high value on personalism and egoistic concerns. Their concern with Prestige, Dignity, Security and Job Satisfaction is much higher than is the case for managers in the other countries. Coupled with a high level of egoistic concern, however, is a relatively low self-evaluation. The concept Me has a lower behavioral relevance score for Indian managers than for any other managers studied. The rated importance of Me is also much lower for Indian managers than for other managers.

It seems probable that the conflict and tension produced by high egoistic concerns and low self-evaluation helps explain why Indian managers as a group value stable organizations with minimal or slow rates of change. Organizational stasis as opposed to organizational flux seems to be the kind of organizational environment that fits the modal value pattern of Indian managers. The rather low degree of interorganizational mobility of Indian managers as seen in their work histories is also consistent with these observations about stability and stasis.

Groups of people in one's organizational environment do not play as significant a part in the value system of Indian managers as is the case with managers from other countries. This same observation has been made by other researchers who used different samples and measurement approaches and is probably a valid observation (Haire et al., 1966; Smith and Thomas, 1972; Negandhi and Prasad, 1971). We have no data to suggest why Indian managers place low relevance on "other groups" but suspect it is a function of the same forces that lead to high egoistic concerns. The degree of social stratification that exists, the dependency relationships that are evident and the competition for egoistic gratification may influence one to view other groups as threatening rather than as supportive.

It seems rather clear that the value systems of Indian managers are related to both their behavior and to their success as managers. The values of the more successful managers in India are similar to those of successful managers in other countries. Successful managers' value systems depart from the modal Indian pattern to a considerable extent. Successful managers in India favor pragmatic, dynamic, achievement-oriented values while less successful managers prefer more static and passive values. It should be remembered, however, that our measure of success is an economic one (relative salary level for one's age group) and as such does not necessarily tap the dimensions underlying other definitions of success. We do not know, for example, how our definition of success would relate to a manager's self-perception of his own success.

A sizeable proportion of Indian managers have value systems that seem to combine the notions of organizational competence and organizational compliance. This is particularly noticeable among managers with higher levels of education and managers in northern India. These managers seem to blend elements of their traditional culture with the demands of modernization to a marked degree. We would characterize these individuals as evolutionary managers as opposed to revolutionary or traditional managers. They are the managers who are apt to produce and deal with realistic change. We view them as contributing greatly to the steady growth and development of management in India.

JAPANESE MANAGERS

The Japanese sample consisted of 374 managers. About two-thirds of the sample were employed in manufacturing companies and there is reasonable representation from the nine job functions or departments. Approximately one-third of the managers came from each size of company category: small—under 1000 employees; medium size—1000 to 4999 employees; and large—5000 and over employees. Fifty-seven percent of the managers were in distinctly top management level jobs, 34 percent were in upper middle management level positions and 6 percent were in lower middle management jobs. Twenty percent were line managers, 34 percent were staff managers and 45 percent reported combined line-staff positions. The median salary for the sample is $9400, the median length of managerial experience is ten years and the median age is 54 years. Japanese managers report a high level of job satisfaction, slightly less than American managers and slightly more than Korean managers.

We classify 67 percent of Japanese managers as having a pragmatic orientation, 10 percent as having a moralistic orientation and 7 percent as having an affect orientation. Japanese managers show the highest degree of pragmatism among the five countries and a very low degree of moralistic orientation (they are most similar to Korean managers in this respect). Japanese managers, then, are almost totally pragmatic in nature and only slightly moralistic in nature. We find that the degree of pragmatism among Japanese managers increasing from small to large size organizations and decreasing from higher to lower level positions within organizations. Primary orientation is not related to type of company (manufacturing versus nonmanufacturing) and is not consistently related to age of the manager.

Figure 5-4 presents the value profile for Japanese managers which shows the behavioral relevance score for each of the 66 concepts in the PVQ and categorizes the concepts into operative values, intended values, adopted values and weak values. The first observation to be made concerns the high degree of overlap in behavioral relevance scores between intended and adopted values. A similar pattern is found for Korean managers and we believe that it indicates that intended values and adopted values may have about equal behavioral significance for these two countries while intended values tend to be more behaviorally significant than adopted values for American, Australian and Indian managers. The reason for this distinction is not readily apparent to us at present. We have viewed this difference and our data from the perspectives of translation problems, the unimodal nature of primary orientations in Japan and Korea, and the possibility of a real and meaningful difference between the two groups of countries (Japan and Korea versus U.S.A., Australia and India). We are not fully satisfied with any one of these possibilities and must leave the question open.

Viewing the operative values in Figure 5-4, a very high degree of internalization of organizational goals is suggested for Japanese managers (higher than in any other country). This is particularly true of magnitude goals (growth

Figure 5-4. Value Profile—Japanese Managers

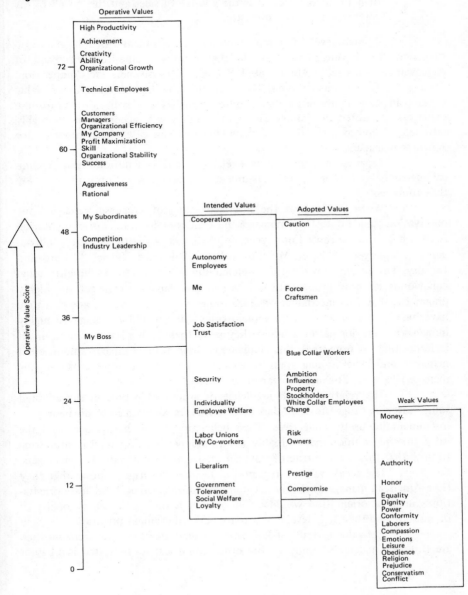

and high productivity). The tendency of Japanese managers to emphasize size and expansion of the firm are in accord with the observations about Japanese managers' behavior by Adams and Kobayashi (1969):

> One of the prime motivations in Japanese life, face-saving, is very much in the mind of Japanese management. That is why maintenance of volume of sales becomes more important to managers than profit on sales. It is the volume of sales and the "size" of the enterprise that are emphasized. . . .

A high level of competence and achievement orientation is also suggested for Japanese managers in the operative value set comprised of Achievement, Creativity, Ability, Skill, Success, Aggressiveness and Competition.

The operative value Rational and the high level adopted value Caution imply a highly rationalized and cautious style of behavior for Japanese managers. As noted in Chapter Three, this finding is in accord with the highly rationalized and consental decision making that has often been reported for Japanese managers.

Japanese managers show a relatively high orientation toward technical personnel as well as to Customers, Managers, My Company and My Subordinates.

When we look at the intended values of Japanese managers, one observation stands out. These managers have an intended humanistic orientation as shown by the concepts Employees, Job Satisfaction, Trust, Security, Individuality, Employee Welfare, My Co-workers, Tolerance, Social Welfare and Loyalty. The extent to which this intended humanism gets translated into actual behavior is certainly problematical. The fact that Japanese managers are highly pragmatic, that they internalize organization goals to a high degree and that they have high competence and achievement orientation would argue against highly humanistic behavior patterns unless they serve these higher level orientations. It is interesting to note that this humanistic orientation is higher among older managers and lower among younger managers and probably represents changing managerial styles of behavior in Japanese management.

The relatively high incidence of groups of people in the adopted value category suggests that Japanese managers view groups of people as instrumentally useful collectives. Their behavior toward these groups and the value they place upon them is highly situation-dependent. Again, it is interesting to note that this is more true of younger managers than it is of older managers.

The weak value category for Japanese managers shows that they (like American managers) clearly reject any organizational egalitarianism orientation. Such an orientation would be in conflict with their organizational goal orientation and their high level competence and achievement orientation.

The value systems of Japanese managers are more homogeneous than are those of managers in any of the other countries. As indicated in Chapter

Three, this finding is historically and culturally understandable and we would be most surprised if our data indicated otherwise. One could certainly speculate that this homogeneity of value patterns and the nature of Japanese value patterns may offer partial explanation of Japan's industrial success.

The Japanese manager value system is at a mid-level of complexity in a factorial sense. Eight factors were found in Japan, more complex than the American or Indian pattern and less complex than the Korean pattern.

Japanese managers differ the most of any of the five countries from the international sample of managers which is comprised of a random sample of 150 managers from each country. We would speculate that Japanese management has imported values as well as technology and blended the importation with their traditional value patterns to a higher degree than have any of our other countries.

The Japanese managerial value system is most like that of Korean managers (although there is no simiarity in factor structure) and least like that of Australian managers.

The value patterns of Japanese managers are related to their success and to their job satisfaction in ways similar to that found in other countries, although success is less predictable by value patterns in Japan than is the case in other countries. Likewise, the common value key for predicting success works least well in Japan among the five countries. While these two results might be a function of the greater homogeneity of Japanese values and the greater dissimilarity of Japanese manager values to those of other country managers, it probably also represents less intrinsic relationship between values and success.

As indicated earlier, it is among Japanese managers where age makes the most difference in values. In Japan, 36 percent of the 66 concepts showed age differences while the other four countries showed age differences on 17 percent of the concepts on the average. We would take this finding as an indication of more rapid value change in Japan than in any other country. This observation is further supported by the fact that Japanese managers are most pragmatic among the five countries and pragmatism implies an easier shift of values when conditions change and/or when change is necessitated.

In summary, the outstanding value characteristics of Japanese managers as a group are:

high level pragmatic orientation,
high level organizational goal orientation,
high level competence and achievement orientation,
intended humanistic orientation,
changing value patterns, and
rejection of organizational egalitarian orientation.

KOREAN MANAGERS

The Korean sample consisted of 211 managers from South Korea. Three-fourths of the sample were employed in manufacturing companies while there was reasonable representation from three other industries. Forty-eight percent of the managers were employed in small organizations—under 500 employees; 27 percent in medium size companies—500-999 employees; and 25 percent in large firms—1000 and over employees. Thirty-four percent of the managers reported their job function as general administration and there was reasonable representation in five other functions. Thirty-nine percent were employed in line positions, 21 percent in staff positions and 39 percent in combined line-staff positions. Fifty-seven percent of the managers were in the top level management jobs, 34 percent were in upper middle management positions and 6 percent were in lower middle management positions. Three-fourths of the sample reported a salary of $3000 or less while about 6 percent reported salaries of $25,000 or over. The median years of managerial experience were 12 years while the median age was 44 years. Korean managers report the lowest job satisfaction among the five countries although job satisfaction is high in an absolute sense.

We classify 53 percent of Korean managers as having a pragmatic orientation, 9 percent as having a moralistic orientation, 9 percent as having an affect orientation and 29 percent as having a mixed orientation. Korean managers, then, are highly pragmatically oriented and only minimally moralistic in orientation. They are similar to Japanese managers in this respect. We find that the degree of pragmatism among Korean managers increases with size of organization, with the level of the manager within the organization and with employment in manufacturing as opposed to nonmanufacturing companies. There is no consistent relationship between primary orientation and age of the manager.

Figure 5-5 presents the value profile for Korean managers which shows the behavioral relevance score for each of the 66 concepts in the PVQ and categorizes the concepts into operative values, intended values, adopted values and weak values.

We note for Korean managers as we did for Japanese managers that there is high overlap in the behavioral relevance scores on intended values and on adopted values. Our puzzlement over this finding can be seen in the preceding section and will not be repeated here.

The set of concepts which are operative values for Korean managers suggest two major observations. First, organizational goal concepts are internalized to a considerable extent for Korean managers. While the relevancy of organizational goals is present, it is lower than that found for Japanese and American managers. Second, the set of operative values (Ability, Success, Achievement, Aggressiveness, Skill, Job Satisfaction and Me) indicates a high level competence and achievement orientation for Korean managers. This is similar to our findings for Japanese and American managers. We think, however,

Figure 5-5. Value Profile—Korean Managers

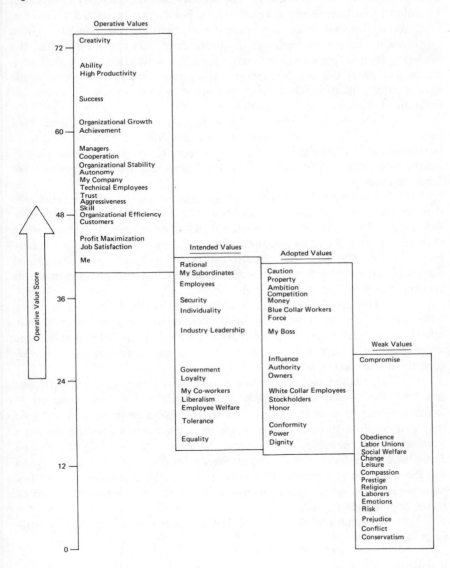

that the competence and achievement orientation is more self-oriented as opposed to organizationally oriented for Korean managers. It is only in Korea that the concept Me is an operative value.

The major conclusion we draw from the intended values of Korean managers is one of an intended egalitarian orientation. The intended value set of concepts (My Subordinates, Employees, Security, Individuality, My Co-workers, Liberalism, Employee Welfare, Tolerance and Equality) suggests such an orientation. As is the case with most intended orientations, the translation from intentionality into actual behavior is problematical. In the present case, the moderate level of organizational goal orientation would seem to permit such translation while the competence and achievement orientation would argue against such translation. On balance, we might expect a moderate amount of egalitarian behavior among Korean managers.

The relatively high incidence of groups of people in the adopted value category suggests that Korean managers view groups of people as instrumentally useful collectives and their behavior toward these groups is highly situation-dependent. This observation was also found to be supported for Japanese managers.

The adopted value category also forms a set of behavioral strategies that are defined by Caution, Competition, Force, Influence, Authority, Conformity and Power. These adopted behavioral strategies are probably used when the situation calls for them and their general influence on behavior is certainly problematical. The fact that Korean managers are highly pragmatic would suggest that the strategies would indeed be used when needed. Korean managers are similar to American managers in this respect.

The set of concepts Change, Risk and Conflict are very weak values, while Compromise has a relatively higher behavioral relevance score. As indicated earlier, we interpret this to imply a cautious, static behavioral strategy which requires a high degree of accommodation or compromise in achieving goals for Korean managers.

Korean managers are most like Japanese managers in value patterns and least like Australian managers. This similarity of Korean managers to Japanese managers must be tempered by the fact that Korean managers are least homogeneous (similarity of one manager to another) while Japanese managers were most homogeneous. Additionally, the factor structures for Korea and Japan were not related. The Korean manager value structure had ten factors and was the most complex among the five countries. This fact coupled with the low homogeneity among Korean managers supports the individualistic or self-directed orientations noted earlier for Korean managers.

In summary, the outstanding value characteristics of Korean managers as a group are:

pragmatic orientation,
self-oriented achievement and competence orientation,
moderate level of organization goal orientation,
intended egalitarian orientation, and
cautious behavioral strategies that require a high degree of accommodation or compromise.

Chapter Six

Value Categories and Value Classification

The present chapter explores the significance of the major value categories which have been used in the preceding analyses. Specifically, we will look at the value systems of pragmatic and moralistic managers and will consider the four major value categories: operative values, intended values, adopted values and weak values. We turn first to a comparison of pragmatic and moralistic managers.

PRAGMATIC VERSUS MORALISTIC MANAGERS

While the procedures and rationale for classifying managers into the primary orientation groups (pragmatic, moralistic, affect and mixed) have been presented earlier, it is of interest to look at the value profile differences between the two major groups (pragmatists and moralists) in terms of the 66 concepts. Such a comparison will show to what extent and in what ways these two orientation groups differ. Table 6-1 presents the concepts where there is a significant difference between the two groups which is consistent in all five countries. The table shows that the two groups differ by 10 percent or more in behavioral relevance score on 33 of the 66 concepts. It also shows that pragmatists and moralists differ on all organizational goals, on over three-fourths of the concepts dealing with ideas associated with people, on nearly half of the personal goal concepts and on one-third or less of the concepts dealing with groups of people and general topics.

These results suggest that the major distinction between the value systems of pragmatists and moralists is one where pragmatists have an economic and organizational competence orientation as opposed to a humanistic bureaucratic orientation for moralists. Pragmatists also display a much higher achievement orientation than do moralists. These generalizations are further supported by the fact that pragmatic managers are slightly more successful, occupy higher level positions and earn higher incomes than do moralists.

Table 6-1.   Concept Differences Between Pragmatists and Moralists

Pragmatists Have Higher Behavioral Relevance Scores than Moralists	*Concept Groups*	*Moralists Have Higher Behavioral Relevance Scores than Pragmatists*
	Organizational Goals	
	8 of 8	
High Productivity (36)*		Employee Welfare (40)
Organizational Growth (34)		Social Welfare (24)
Profit Maximization (32)		
Organizational Efficiency (17)		
Organizational Stability (14)		
Industry Leadership (12)		
	Ideas Associated with People	
	10 of 13	
Ability (39)		Trust (52)
Aggressiveness (26)		Loyalty (51)
Skill (19)		Honor (46)
Ambition (18)		Tolerance (25)
		Compassion (25)
		Obedience (25)
	Personal Goals	
	6 of 13	
Success (39)		Dignity (38)
Achievement (35)		Security (15)
Creativity (24)		
Money (18)		
	General Concepts	
	5 of 15	
Change (13)		Religion (28)
		Equality (25)
		Authority (17)
		Liberalism (16)
	Groups of People	
	4 of 17	
Managers (19)		Government (26)
Customers (15)		
My Company (11)		

*The difference in behavioral relevance score between the two groups in the international sample.

Table 6-2 shows that pragmatists are slightly more successful than moralists, pragmatists have more homogeneous value systems than do moralists and that the two groups do not differ in reported job satisfaction scores. This latter fact is consistent with the finding of no difference between the two groups on the concept Job Satisfaction, the behavioral relevance scores being 56 for pragmatists and 53 for moralists. As noted in Table 6-2, pragmatists tend to be more successful than do moralists except in Japan where the opposite is true. It should be remembered from Chapter Four that we were least able to predict managerial success from specially developed value keys in Japan among the five countries. Again, we note that the relationship between success and values is different for Japanese managers than is the case in the other countries.

The finding of greater homogeneity among pragmatists than among moralists takes on added significance when it is viewed against the broader perspective of these two value categories. The notion of primary value orientation has been used in the present study as a motivational behavior linking construct. It describes the overall evaluative framework which an individual utilizes in making decisions.

For managers with moralistic value orientations, the evaluative framework consists of ethical considerations channeling managerial behavior toward actions and decisions which are judged to be "right." On the other hand, pragmatic managers are guided primarily in their behavior by success-failure considerations. Thus they would choose to act in a particular way if it were judged to lead to success. Besides differing in the considerations that influence managerial behavior, the two evaluative frameworks also differ in another important way. This relates to the degree of subjectivity or objectivity of the considerations themselves. It can be argued that ethical standards signifying what is considered to be "right" are highly subjective and therefore permit great person to person variability. In contrast to this, an individual's perception of what he considers to be successful is likely to be more objective insofar as it is based on factors such as personal-organizational income, growth, assets and relative position in the organizational or industrial hierarchy. Our finding of greater homogeneity among pragmatists than among moralists supports this distinction. It may also be argued that ethical norms are more firmly ingrained in the individual's personality than success standards, thereby rendering the former less amenable to change. If the preceding line of reasoning is valid, organizations would find it easier to modify behavior patterns of pragmatic rather than moralistic managers. Not only would a more individualistic program of behavior modification be required for moralistic managers but such a program also would need to be on a more intensified scale. We would also expect that the primary orientation of managers would make them differentially sensitive to training and educational approaches utilizing different underlying rationales and reasoning. Moralists would likely to be more influenced by positions and approaches utilizing philosophical and moral justification while pragmatists would be more influenced by practical arguments and approaches finding support in whether or not a particular act or decision will work or is likely to be successful. The notion

Table 6-2.   Pragmatist-Moralist Comparisons

Variable	Primary Orientation Group	International Sample	U.S.A.	Japan	Korea	Australia	India
Percent of Group in the Top Half of Success Index	Pragmatists	52	55	37	—	59	53
	Moralists	49	49	44	—	43	47
Homogeneity Index	Pragmatists	0.90	0.81	0.77	0.94	0.84	0.91
	Moralists	1.01	0.93	0.83	0.95	0.92	0.95
Job Satisfaction Scores	Pragmatists	21.4	22.7	21.5	19.9	21.3	22.0
	Moralists	21.5	22.6	21.4	20.2	20.9	21.7

of expected economic outcomes of actions would seem more central to pragmatists than to moralists while the reverse would be true for the notion of expected human outcomes of actions. It must, of course, be pointed out here that the above assertions need further empirical investigation.

In summary, we used the construct of primary orientation as a means for determining the value system of an individual or a group. The essential rationale was to shred out some of the intentionality in value statements in an effort to get closer to the behavioral significance of values. We find that it indeed serves this function. Additionally, we find major value differences between managers having the two most frequent primary orientations—pragmatists and moralists. Pragmatists display an economic and organizational competence and achievement orientation while moralists have a humanistic bureaucratic orientation. We further believe that a pragmatic orientation is more readily changed and/or able to deal with change than is a moralistic orientation. It would seem that Japanese, Korean and American managers are likely to be more change-oriented while Indian and Australian managers are less change-oriented.

OPERATIVE VALUES

Operative values are defined theoretically as those which a manager views as important and which fit his primary value orientation. For pragmatists, they are defined by those concepts viewed as important and successful; for moralists, they are defined by those concepts viewed as important and right; and for affect-oriented individuals, they are defined by those concepts viewed as important and pleasant. Both our theory and our results indicate that operative values are those which best indicate likely behavior; they are most likely to be translated from the intentional value state into behavior. We have defined operative values empirically for managers in each country in Chapter Four and attempt integration of these results here.

Of the 66 concepts in the PVQ, 23 are operative values in the United States, 22 are operative values in Australia and India, and 20 are operative values in Japan and Korea. Thus, in terms of number of operative values, there is little difference among the five countries.

The range of behavioral relevance scores of operative value concepts among the five countries is from 33 to 79, while the median value is 59. Thus, there is a considerable degree of variability in the behavioral relevance scores of those concepts that are classified as operative values in the five countries.

There are nine concepts that are operative values in all five countries and an additional five concepts that are operative values in four of the five countries. We shall use these 14 concepts to empirically define operative values for our total sample of 2500 managers. Table 6-2 lists these 14 concepts by concept category.

Table 6-3 shows that across the five countries stability, productivity

Table 6-3.   Operative Values for Total Sample of Managers

Concept Category	Operative Value Concepts
Organizational Goals	Organizational Stability
	High Productivity
	Organizational Efficiency
Personal Goals of Individuals	Achievement
	Creativity
	Success
	Job Satisfaction
Ideas Associated with People	Ability
	Skill
	Cooperation
Groups of People and Institutions	My Company
	Customers
	Technical Employees
	Managers

and efficiency are the organizational goals that are being commonly sought. The personal goals of managers across the five countries might best be described as self-actualization or achievement-oriented goals; these appear to be the goals for which managers are striving. The set of concepts defined by Ability, Skill and Cooperation are the traits or characteristics that are most highly valued by these managers and they indicate a competence orientation. Finally, the most relevant groups of people for the managers in the five countries show identification with their own company and its customers and with managerial and technical personnel. These are the groups with which managers identify most highly and it is these groups that serve as relevant reference groups in the behavior of these managers.

In summary, the operative values for managers in the five countries are those that will most influence their behavior. These operative values show an organizational goal orientation, a self-actualization and achievement orientation, a competence orientation and an orientation toward high level managerial and technical personnel within the organization and with customers of the organization.

INTENDED VALUES

Intended values have been defined theoretically as those which a manager views as important but which do not fit his primary orientation. For pragmatists, they are defined by those concepts viewed as important and right or pleasant; for moralists, they are defined by those concepts viewed as important and successful or pleasant; and for affect-oriented individuals, they are defined by those concepts viewed as important and successful or right. Our theory suggests that intended values have a high level of intentionality but their translation into behavior is problematical and depends largely on whether or not the specific situation in which they might influence behavior is controlled by the more powerful orientations stemming from operative values. In short, intended values will influence behavior when they are supportive or at least not in conflict with operative values but not in situations where they are antagonistic to operative values.

Of the 66 concepts in the PVQ, 11 are intended values in the United States, Australia and India, 13 are intended values in Korea and 16 in Japan. Again, we see a relatively small difference among the five countries in terms of the number of intended values.

The range of behavioral relevance scores of intended value concepts among the five countries is from 11 to 49 with a median score of 38. There is considerable variation in the behavioral relevance scores of those concepts that are classified as intended values in the five countries.

There are only three concepts that are intended values in all five countries and an additional two concepts that are intended values in four of the five countries. These five concepts are Employee Welfare, My Co-workers, Government Security and Individuality. Managers seem to be indicating that these concepts are important to them but that their translation from the intentional value state into behavior is problematical. Employee Welfare is viewed as an intended value for managers; they would desire to behave in accordance with Employee Welfare concerns but their organizational experience has not reinforced such behavior to any large extent in the past. Thus, Employee Welfare would not be a behaviorally significant organizational goal if it were in conflict with organizational goals in the operative set of values or unless such behavior is required by forces outside of the organization such as laws or union pressures.

In a similar vein, managers identify with their Co-workers and Government in a positive fashion but their behavior may not be consistent with these identifications. Likewise, the personal goal of Security and the characteristic of Individuality have high degrees of intentionality but behavior that is consistent with these intentionalities is problematical.

In summary, the intended values for managers show less similarity across the five countries than was the case for operative values. There is also less person to person similarity in intended value than was the case for operative values. The average deviation score for the 14 concepts in the operative value set is .735 while the average deviation score for the five concepts in the intended value category is 1.32. We believe that this greater heterogeneity among intended values stems from the fact that intended values are largely socioculturally induced. Since we are dealing with countries with quite different social and cultural patterns and since it is these patterns that seem to generate intended values to a large extent, we would expect and we observe considerable country variation among intended values.

We also believe, but have no real proof, that intended values may indicate areas where there is likely to be conflict between what one has learned to believe (or to value) in his total life space and what he finds workable or present in his organizational environment. If this is the case, our intended values suggest that managers would show the most value conflict about the treatment of other people, about the degree of individuality that one can express in his organizational role and about the security of one's place in the organization.

ADOPTED VALUES

Adopted values are defined by the set of concepts that are not viewed as important by a manager but which fit his primary orientation. Theoretically, we view adopted values as being less a part of the personality structure of the individual and they would affect behavior largely because of situational factors. They are defined for pragmatists by concepts viewed as successful but not important, right but not important for moralists and pleasant but not important for affect-oriented individuals.

Of the 66 concepts in the PVQ, 18 are adopted values for Korean managers; 14 are adopted values in Japan, Australia and India; and 13 are adopted values for American managers. Again, we see little difference among the countries in the number of adopted values.

The range of behavioral relevance scores of adopted value concepts among the five countries is from 11 to 47 with a median value of 27. There is considerable variation in behavioral relevance scores of adopted value concepts among the five countries.

There are only three concepts which are adopted values in all five countries and an additional five concepts that are adopted values in four of the five countries. These eight concepts are White Collar Employees, Blue Collar Workers, Craftsmen, Stockholders, Property, Authority, Change and Risk. These concepts would seem to represent two sets. One set is composed of groups of individuals who are not viewed as important in their own right by managers but who may be viewed as instrumentally useful groups to managers in achieving their goals. The second set of adopted value concepts can be interpreted as a set of behavioral strategies (use of authority, risk taking, change) which have been reinforced in the managers' organizational experience. They are not desired or desirable in and of themselves but have been shown to be useful in the past and would be called upon if the situation required it.

There is moderate agreement (less than for operative values but more than for intended values) among the five countries on the concepts that are adopted values. The average deviation score for the eight adopted value concepts is 1.21. Adopted values, for our total sample of managers, indicate an instrumentally useful set of groups of people and point to a set of behavioral strategies. The translation of these orientations into behavior is problematical and would seem to depend upon the situation.

WEAK VALUES

Weak values are defined by that set of concepts which are viewed as neither important by a manager nor fitting his primary orientation. Theoretically, we see them as influencing behavior only marginally.

Of the 66 concepts in the PVQ, 19 are weak values in the United States, Australia and India, 16 in Japan and 15 in Korea. Again, we find little difference among the five countries in the number of concepts that are weak values.

The range of behavioral relevance scores of weak value concepts among the five countries is from one to 27 with a median value of 14. There are six concepts which represent weak values in all five countries and an additional three concepts that are weak values for four of the five countries. These nine concepts are Equality, Compassion, Social Welfare, Religion, Emotions, Conflict, Leisure, Conservatism and Prejudice. The outstanding characteristic of this set of concepts is the rejection by managers of egalitarianism. Such an egalitarian orientation would be in direct conflict with the higher order orientation of managers toward organizational and individual competence and is clearly rejected. The nature of management jobs, the selection process that managers go through and their own value orientations argue strongly against any orientation toward egalitarianism. As noted many times earlier, managers are most often pragmatic in their outlook.

The value types and classifications presented in this chapter do provide meaningful methods of inferring expected behavior. In short, they are helpful in understanding managers, their values and their behavior.

Chapter Seven

Value Knowledge About the Individual

The preceding chapters have dealt with the personal value systems of managers in terms of primary value orientations, value profiles and expected behavior. These forms of analyses are aggregative in nature and tell us little about questions of individual differences in values or about the values of any specific individual. The present chapter focuses on individual differences and upon what value information we can obtain for any individual.

POTENTIAL INFORMATION ABOUT
THE INDIVIDUAL

For illustrative purposes, we have selected an American manager whose individual value profile is not atypical to any large extent from that of the overall American manager value profile. As pointed out earlier, the approach we have developed identifies four alternative value categories in which a concept may be placed by an individual: operative, intended, adopted and weak. The behavioral relevance or significance of these categories of values varies directly in the order they are mentioned, operative values being of most behavioral relevance and weak values of least behavioral significance.

Figure 7-1 presents the value profile or value matrix for one American Manager, Number 901. According to our decision rules (see Appendix C for a detailed presentation of these rules), we would classify this manager as a pragmatist because he tends to view those concepts which are high in importance as successful to a greater extent than he views them as right or as pleasant. The first bit of information we have about Manager 901, then, is that he is a pragmatist. Based on the knowledge that Manager 901 is a pragmatist, we can next categorize his concepts into operative, intended, adopted and weak values as shown in Figure 7-1. Next we can be concerned about the degree or extent to which Manager 901 is a pragmatist. Two scores can be used to present this

Figure 7-1.   Individual Value Profile (Value Profile for Manager 901)

	Concepts Viewed as Successful	Concepts Viewed as Right	Concepts Viewed as Pleasant	
Concepts Rated High in Importance	Organizational Efficiency High Productivity Profit Maximization Organizational Growth Organizational Stability Achievement Creativity Success Job Satisfaction Influence Ambition Ability Aggressiveness Skill Authority ┌ Operative ┐ Change └ Values ┘ Competition Rational Risk P (Ext.) = .36, My Company 73% Customers Me P (Int.) = .63, Managers 64% Owners	Employee Welfare Dignity Individuality Cooperation Trust Loyalty Honor Religion My Co-workers Craftsmen Government ┌─────────────┐ └ Intended Values ┘ P (Intended) = .21, 50%	Industry Leadership Money Property	P(HI) = .58 72%
Concepts Rated Not High in Importance	Prejudice Caution Compromise Conflict Force Employees Technical Employees	Autonomy Obedience Compassion Tolerance Conservatism My Boss My Subordinates Stockholders White Collar Employees	Social Welfare Prestige Leisure Security Power Conformity Emotions Equality Liberalism Laborers Blue Collar Workers Labor Unions	— P(HI) = .42 42%
	┌ Adopted Values ┐ P (Adopted) = .11, 34%	┌ Weak Values ┐ P (Weak) = .32, 55%		
	P (S) = .47, 57%	P (R) = .30, 37%	P (P) = .23, 59%	

information: extensiveness of pragmatic orientation and intensiveness of pragmatic orientation. We note that Manager 901 places 24 concepts in his operative value category; thus his extensiveness of pragmatic orientation can be expressed as a probability score—P(Successful and High Importance). This extensiveness score would be 24/66 or .36. We can next compare this extensiveness score to that of all American managers, and find that the extensiveness of pragmatic orientation for Manager 901 is at the 73rd percentile for American managers. Twenty-seven percent of American managers have a higher pragmatic extensiveness score and 73 percent have a lower extensiveness score. This score (as its name implies) indicates the scope or extensiveness of the individual's pragmatic orientation over all of the 66 concepts. The larger the number of concepts in the operative value set, the wider the scope of the manager's primary orientation (a pragmatic orientation in our example). The intensiveness of pragmatic orientation for Manager 901 is obtained by determining the extent to which he classifies high importance concepts as successful. The intensiveness score (expressed as a probability) for Manager 901 would be P(Successful and High Importance), 24/38 or .63. Again, we can compare the score obtained with that of all American managers and find that the intensiveness of pragmatic orientation for Manager 901 is at the 64th percentile. The intensiveness score indicates the extent to which the manager views all high importance concepts in a pragmatic way.

Next, we can show that the probability of intended values for Manager 901 is 14/66 or .21, the probability of adopted values is 7/66 or .11, and the probability of weak values is 21/66 or .32. Again, we can relate these scores to our total American sample and find that the percentile scores are 50, 34 and 55 respectively.

We can also note that Manager 901 views 38 of the 66 concepts as being of high importance. The P(High Importance) is thus 38/66 or .58. This High Importance Probability is at the 72nd percentile for American managers. Finally, we can note the extent to which Manager 901 uses each of the secondary orientations (successful, right and pleasant). These values for Manager 901 are P(Successful) = .47, P(Right) = .30, and P(Pleasant) = .23. The respective percentiles for these scores are 57, 37 and 59 when we compare them to all American managers.

Let us then summarize this quantitative information about Manager 901 before looking at the content of the concepts placed in each category:

He is a pragmatist.
His extensiveness of pragmatism is at the 73rd percentile for American managers.
His intensiveness of pragmatism is also relatively high, at the 64th percentile.
He views a high proportion of concepts as important (.58 of them) which places him at the 72nd percentile.
His intended values comprise .21 of all concepts which is an average proportion compared to all American managers (50th percentile).
His set of adopted values is small, being at the 34th percentile.
His set of weak values comprises .32 of the 66 concepts and represents the 55th percentile.
His overall use of the successful orientation is at the 57th percentile, his use of

the right orientation is at the 37th percentile, while his use of the pleasant orientation is at the 59th percentile.

When we combine this quantitative information about Manager 901 with the content of the concepts which are operative, intended, adopted and weak values for him, we obtain the following description of his value system:

high degree of pragmatism,
relatively high degree of intended orientations,
internalizes organizational goals highly and shows high organizational identification,
shows a high level of achievement and competence orientation,
shows a high degree of action orientation,
shows an intended humanistic orientation whose translation into behavior is problematical,
will probably experience conflict about the treatment of people within the organization,
shows an adopted orientation toward a set of behavioral strategies defined by Prejudice, Caution, Compromise, Force and Conflict (these strategies will probably be used when the situation requires them), and
rejects organizational egalitarianism.

In total, we believe that we obtain a considerable amount of value information about the individual which is useful in understanding his value system and its impact upon his behavior.

INDIVIDUAL VARIABILITY IN VALUE PROFILES

The individual variability in value profiles can be most readily seen when we look at how a number of individual managers view the 66 concepts in the PVQ. We have selected a number of cases to show the range of individual differences in values. Tables 7-1 and 7-2 present data on the frequency of concepts in the operative, intended, adopted and weak value categories for 14 managers.

Table 7-1 shows a summary of the values of four individual managers. The personal value systems of the first two managers (A and B) are comprised almost totally of operative values and imply that a large number of concepts are not only regarded as highly important but also fit each individual's primary value orientation. In contrast to these are managers C and D whose personal value systems consist of a minimum number of operative values. According to the decision rules used in the present study, an individual's primary orientation is regarded as mixed if the number of operative values for him falls below ten (i.e., 15 percent of the concepts). This number is viewed as a

Table 7-1.   Number of Operative and Nonoperative Values for Selected Managers

Manager	Primary Value Orientation	Number of Operative Values	Number of Nonoperative Values
A	Pragmatic	56	10
B	Moralistic	55	11
C	Pragmatic	10	56
D	Moralistic	10	56

minimum for any meaningful behavioral generalizations to be drawn from one's personal value profile. Thus, fewer concepts in the PVQ imply strong behavioral significance for managers C and D.

Table 7-2 presents additional data on individual differences in values. The first set of cases (E to H) depicts personal value systems which are comprised largely of only one type of values. Thus, manager E's personal value system contains a very high proportion of operative values. In contrast to this, adopted, intended and weak values appear to dominate the personal value systems of managers F, G and H respectively. The next four cases (I to L) share concentration in two (but varying) categories of values. For example, a high majority of the 66 concepts appear as either operative or adopted values for manager I; operative or intended values for manager J; operative or weak values for manager K; and adopted or weak values for manager L. Finally, managers M

Table 7-2.   Number of Operative, Intended, Adopted and Weak Values for Selected Managers

Manager	Primary Value Orientation	Operative Values	Intended Values	Adopted Values	Weak Values
E	Moralistic	55	6	2	3
F	Pragmatic	12	5	33	16
G	Moralistic	14	41	1	10
H	Moralistic	14	5	1	46
I	Moralistic	30	4	27	5
J	Pragmatic	30	35	0	1
K	Pragmatic	27	1	0	38
L	Moralistic	13	7	23	23
M	Pragmatic	19	13	15	19
N	Moralistic	18	0	0	48

and N show contrasting situations in which one has a fairly even distribution of the 66 concepts across the four value categories while the other has a very truncated distribution.

Apart from the quantitative differences pointed out above, there also are significant variations in the content of individual personal value systems. Content refers to the meaning of the concepts as opposed to their number. Quantitatively, two managers may have identical numbers of operative and other types of values and still differ in terms of which concepts constitute those sets. To illustrate these differences, several contrasts are presented in Figures 7-2 through 7-4.

Figure 7-2 involves managers C and D who, as shown in Table 7-1, have an identical number of operative and nonoperative values. For the sake of simplicity of exposition, only the operative value sets of these managers are compared here. It appears that manager C's operative value set consists primarily of company-related goals, organizationally relevant groups of people and competence-oriented notions. In contrast to this, operative values of manager D represent concepts largely of personalistic and compliance dimensions. To a large extent, the same contrast is true between managers O and P (Figure 7-3). Finally, Figure 7-4 shows four managers who have divergent value profiles with respect to organizational and personal goals. For example, all but one concept in these two categories are operative values for manager O while the same concepts are primarily weak values for manager T. Similarly, the value profiles of managers R and S are quite distinct from each other. For the former, all organizational goals are operative values and all personal goals are nonoperative values. For the latter, however, just the opposite is true.

The examples shown illustrate the large range of individual differences that are found in the value profiles of managers within each group we have

Figure 7-2.   Operative Value Sets for Managers C and D

Operative Values		
Exclusive to C	Exclusive to D	Common to both C and D
Organizational Stability	Industry Leadership	My Subordinates
Profit Maximization	Me	Technical Employees
Customers	Trust	
Craftsmen	Loyalty	
Blue Collar Workers	Honor	
My Company	Dignity	
Ability	Competition	
Skill	Liberalism	

Figure 7-3. Operative Value Sets for Managers O and P

Operative Values		
Exclusive to O	Exclusive to P	Common to both O and P
Industry Leadership	Employee Welfare	High Productivity
Organizational Efficiency	Craftsmen	Organizational Growth
Ambition	Technical Employees	
Ability	Dignity	
Skill	Individuality	
Achievement	Job Satisfaction	
Creativity	Power	
Success	Rational	

studied. Among managers in each country, some have a pragmatic orientation (they view ideas and concepts in terms of whether or not they work or are successful), some have an ethical-moral orientation (they view ideas in terms of being right or wrong), while a few have an affect or feeling orientation (they view ideas in terms of whether or not they are pleasant). Some managers have a very small set of operative values while others have a large set and seem to be influenced by many strongly held values. The significant values of some managers include concepts which are almost solely related to their organizational life while other managers include a wide range of personal and philosophical concepts among their important values. Some managers have individualistic values as opposed to group-oriented values. Some managers are highly achievement-oriented as opposed to others who value status and prestige more highly. Some managers are humanistic in orientation while others are competence-oriented and reject egalitarianism. Some indicate many intended values which probably cause considerable value conflict while others evidence only minimal value conflict. Personal value systems, then, are like most other human characteristics—individuals differ greatly with respect to them.

Figure 7-4. Categorization of Organizational and Personal Goals for Four Managers

Concepts	Manager Q	Manager R	Manager S	Manager T
Organizational Goals				
High Productivity	O	O	W	I
Industry Leadership	O	O	W	W
Employee Welfare	O	O	A	W
Organizational Stability	O	O	A	I
Profit Maximization	O	O	W	W
Organizational Efficiency	O	O	A	O
Social Welfare	O	O	W	A
Organizational Growth	O	O	A	A
Personal Goals				
Leisure	O	W	O	W
Dignity	O	W	O	W
Achievement	O	W	O	W
Autonomy	O	W	O	W
Money	O	I	O	W
Individuality	W	I	O	W
Job Satisfaction	O	A	O	O
Influence	O	W	O	I
Security	O	W	O	W
Power	O	W	O	W
Creativity	O	W	O	A
Success	O	W	O	W
Prestige	O	I	O	W

Note: In the above figure, O, I, A and W stand for operative, intended, adopted and weak respectively.

Chapter Eight

Implications and the Future

While there are many forms that this concluding chapter could take, we have chosen to structure it around three questions: (1) What have we learned about value assessment in general? (2) What substantive results emerge from our studies? (3) What are important future areas of investigation about managerial values? The reader will certainly note that we are selecting, interpreting, summarizing and inferring in treating these three questions. This process is both necessary and useful and we have made a serious effort to do it in a reasonable manner. One would be naive, however, if he didn't recognize a likely bias toward overestimating the importance of his own work. Fortunately, this bias undoubtedly will be corrected by the critical powers of the reader.

WHAT HAVE WE LEARNED ABOUT VALUE ASSESSMENT IN GENERAL?

We believe that our theory and methodology are a useful addition to the value measurement literature. Managerial values are measurable in different countries through the use of our procedures and are apparently stable enough over time to warrant measurement efforts. More importantly, managerial values as assessed by our procedures are related to important outcomes such as decision making and problem solving, personal success of managers and their levels of job satisfaction. We have demonstrated that the use of a quasi-projective device (such as the PVQ) retains sufficient structure to make results interpretable both within a country and across countries. Finally, our approach is relatively successful in shredding out some of the intentionality in value statements and moving them closer to behavioral outcomes. An example of this shredding effect is seen in the American manager results on the organizational goal concept, Employee Welfare. Sixty-six percent of American managers say Employee Welfare is a highly important organizational goal but it is an operative value (high in importance and fits the individuals' primary orientation) for only 34 percent of American managers. The latter figure is much more indicative of actual behavior than is the former figure. The use of some similar type of intentionality shredding would seem to be important in many areas of human assessment where intentionality and actual behavior may be quite different.

The outcome of our research that has the most theoretical relevance and usefulness is the demonstration that values are indeed related to behavior in systematic ways. Methodologically, the most useful aspect of our research is the development of a methodology that shreds out some of the intentionality of value statements and moves them closer to actual behavior. In short, we believe the PVQ methodology provides valid and meaningful information about a manager's values which can be interpreted behaviorally.

WHAT SUBSTANTIVE RESULTS EMERGE FROM OUR STUDIES?

The results of the analyses reported certainly suggest that it is an oversimplification to say that the value systems in the five countries are similar or to say the opposite, that they are very different. Both similarity and difference are exhibited and we must consider both. First, it was noted that there was considerable variation in the primary orientations of managers in the five countries. The extent of pragmatic orientation was highest in Japan and lowest in India. The extent of moralistic orientation was highest in India and lowest in Korea. These differences, however, should be placed in the context of primary orientation similarity among the countries. At least 34 percent of the managers in each country were pragmatists, at least 9 percent in each country were moralists, at least 1 percent in each country were affect-oriented and at least 11 percent in each country had a mixed orientation. This suggests a primary orientation similarity for about 55 percent of the managers across all five countries.

Next, it was noted that there were significant differences in operative value scores on 29 percent of the possible country-concept pairings. This figure is much greater than the 5 percent of differences that we would expect by chance if the countries were not different at all, but it is much lower than the 100 percent of differences one would get if there was complete difference between the countries on each of the 66 concepts. Again, we have significant and meaningful differences but we have similarity as well.

When one correlates the operative value score on the 66 concepts for the five countries, the correlations range from .95 (U.S.A. and Australia) to .64 (Australia-Japan and Australia-Korea). The median correlation for the ten country pairs is .74. A correlation of .74 indicates that 55 percent of the variance is common between the two sets correlated. Thus, we could say, that on the average, 55 percent of the variance is common between any two pairs of countries.

Factor analysis of each country's data resulted in from six to ten factors in each country. The United States and India had the least factors while Korea had the most. About 15 percent of the possible factor comparisons from country to country had a reasonable degree of similarity. Again, we have some similarity but certainly more dissimilarity.

There are differences in the homogeneity of value systems within the five countries. Japanese managers are most similar to each other in this respect, having an average deviation score of .83 on the 66 concepts while Korean managers are most dissimilar to each other, having an average deviation score of 1.01 on the 66 concepts.

Viewing all of our results, it seems that countries are contributing from 30 to 45 percent to the variability we find while individuals are contributing from 55 to 70 percent. Thus we might say that individual differences account for about two-thirds of the variations in value systems of managers while country differences account for about one-third of the variations in value systems of managers in the five countries studied.

The value differences between managers in the five countries and the value diversity within each country do not overshadow the important fact that there is a common pattern of translation of values into behavior and behavior outcomes across the countries. Figure 8-1 shows the type of relationships between managerial values and various organizational, personal and behavioral variables. Organizational level, personal success, decision-making behavior and job satisfaction are related to value patterns in ways which permit generalization across countries and in this sense are most generally useful. Organizational size and the personal variable age are related to values of managers but in a country-specific fashion, thus permitting statements only within a given country about how values and these variables are related. The type of industry in which a manager is employed is not related to values either across countries or within any given country, thus permitting only a statement of no relationship between values and the variable industry. Among all of these relationships, the important generalization that emerges is that values get translated from states of intentionality into behavior and behavior outcomes in a similar way across countries. If such were not the case, comparative studies would remain essentially a group of single country studies with little generalization possibility in a comparative sense. Our results argue strongly for the possibility of generalization across countries and for the real value of comparative studies.

Another major substantive finding concerns the distinction between managers with different primary orientations, particularly the distinction between managers who have a pragmatic orientation and those having a moralistic orientation. As discussed earlier, this distinction is important in a number of ways. First, there is a real difference in the value patterns of the two types of managers. Pragmatists have an economic and organizational competence orientation as opposed to a humanistic bureaucratic orientation for moralists. Pragmatists will be more responsive to the economic aspects of behavior and decisions

Figure 8-1. Relationship of Values to Organizational, Personal and Behavioral Variables

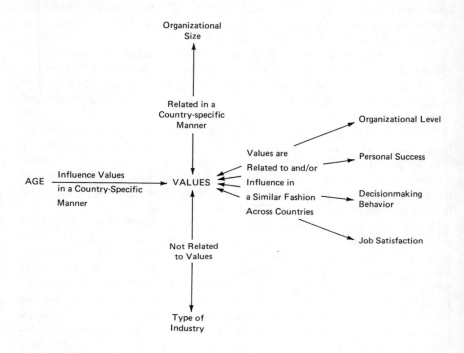

while moralists will be more responsive to the human and bureaucratic consequences of actions. Second, pragmatists are apt to be influenced more by training, persuasion and leadership approaches which focus on the notion of whether or not a particular act or decision will work or is likely to be successful. Moralists, on the other hand, would be more influenced by positions and approaches utilizing philosophical and moral justification. Even should the two types behave in a similar fashion, they would probably rationalize and/or explain the reasons for their behavior in different terms. Third, pragmatists probably have more "situational anchors" to guide their behavior and seem to be more responsive to external rewards and controls while moralists are more responsive to internal rewards and controls. Moral and ethical norms, even though they are more subjective and more variable, are probably more firmly ingrained in the individual's personality than are success standards. Thus, it would be more difficult to change the behavior pattern of a moralist than a pragmatist. In short, we are arguing that the concept of a personal primary orientation for a manager is useful not only in shredding out intentionality in value statements but that the different orientations (particularly pragmatic and moralistic) have important implications for stimulus material selectivity, effectiveness of intervention techniques and change efforts. It is no accident that over half of all the managers we studied have pragmatic orientations.

The fact that India and Australia have the largest proportion of moralistic managers would suggest that change in managers is apt to be slower and/or more difficult in these two countries. This would seem particularly true in India where there are very few value differences between younger and older managers thus providing very little internal management stimulus toward change.

The value systems of Japanese managers were found to be the most homogeneous of all countries. (Whitehill and Takezawa [1968] likewise found more homogeneity in values and attitudes among Japanese production workers than among American production workers.) Japanese managers were also found to be the most pragmatic of all countries and to have the greatest value differences between younger and older managers. All of these factors would indicate a high degree of readiness for change by Japanese managers, when and if such change is necessary. Indeed, such change may well be taking place currently; in any event, Japanese managers seem well prepared for change in terms of their value systems.

Affect-oriented managers (those viewing important concepts as pleasant) are relatively few in each of the five countries, and are the least successful and least satisfied of the orientation groups. Only 36 percent of the affect-oriented managers are in the top half of our success measure as compared to 52 percent of pragmatists and 49 percent of moralists in the international sample. Likewise, the average job satisfaction score for affect-oriented managers is 20.2 as compared to 21.4 for pragmatists and 21.5 for moralists. We are not certain if these lower success and satisfaction levels for affect-oriented managers are a function of their primary orientation per se or if they come about because affect-oriented managers form such a small part of the total management group that their values find little support from the predominant orientation groups (pragmatists and moralists). Whatever the explanation, it is clear that the affect-oriented managers are at a disadvantage in terms of success and satisfaction.

A final set of observations deals with questions of organization and management of tomorrow. Do our results suggest a movement toward such "ideal" forms of organization design as Likert's Management System 4 (1967)? As a guide to this analysis, we have assumed that tomorrow's cadre of important and influential managers will come primarily from the younger age group in our sample. They are already managers but have 25 to 35 years of their career ahead of them. With this fact in mind, we have compared the value systems of younger managers in the international sample with those of older managers to search for clues about the future. While many of the age differences found are country-specific (as noted in Chapter Four), there are a few trends at the international level which are relevant to our present concern:

Young managers place less relevance on organizational goals.
Younger managers place less relevance on groups of people with whom they interact and greater relevance upon themselves (Me).
Younger managers place lower relevance on Trust and Honor.
Younger managers place greater relevance on Money, Ambition and Risk.
Younger managers are slightly more pragmatic than are older managers.

None of these differences indicate any strong or likely movement toward Management System 4; in fact, most of the differences would seem to be in contradiction to such movement. Thus, in terms of the value systems of managers themselves, we would not forecast movement toward ideal types of organization and management such as Likert has proposed. While one can doubt that there will be management initiative for change toward System 4, it is also useful to remember that many managers are pragmatic individuals and can adapt to whatever system seems most appropriate to their circumstances. The notion of situational organizational design would seem to be most in accord with the value systems of managers of the future.

WHAT ARE IMPORTANT FUTURE AREAS OF INVESTIGATION ABOUT MANAGERIAL VALUES?

Data resulting from administration of the PVQ can be utilized for a variety of meaningful research efforts. We shall sketch several possible lines of study that seem most relevant to us.

At the level of the individual, PVQ data can be utilized in understanding an individual's personal value system and the extent to which it may influence his decision-making or leadership style. For this purpose, suitable behavioral measures have to be developed to collect the type of behavior data that is desired. Superior evaluation, peer evaluation, subordinate evaluation and self-evaluation of behavior and performance dimensions as well as objective performance data would all seem to be involved in this effort. The type of value information and behavioral inferences that can be made for an individual from the PVQ are suggested in Chapter Seven. The relationship of this information to actual behavior and performance data would seem a fruitful line of investigation.

Another related question involves studying the relationship between the personal value system of an individual and the type of information that will influence his decision making. Laboratory experimentation would seem the best method of study for this type of question and might proceed as follows:

Decision   As a manager of a firm, you would like to achieve a certain
            goal. You have the option of taking Action A or not taking
            Action A. Would you take Action A or not?

Experimentally controlled situation	Probability that the goal will be achieved if you take Action A	Probability that some long tenured employees will be terminated if you take Action A
	Low High	Low High

(Vary these two probabilities systematically and see whether or not a person takes Action A)

Expectation   Pragmatists will emphasize goal achievement information while moralists will emphasize outcome to employees information.

It seems likely that a substantial number of similar experimental studies could be developed to test our basic assertion that values are related to the type of stimulus material that one will be sensitive to and/or influenced by. We have made only a modest beginning in this line of inquiry.

One may also use PVQ data in assessing the impact of different kinds of training (specific or general) on an individual's values. This could be accomplished by administering the PVQ before and after training. Our theoretical expectation would suggest that only very long-term, intensive and individually designed training efforts would alter value patterns to any significant degree. These, however, are only expectations and not empirical results.

We also know very little about the impact upon an experienced manager of providing him with valid information about his own values. This particular type of self-awareness might be a useful adjunct in sensitivity training efforts in countering some of the negative and damaging outcomes from such training. In any event, the goal of obtaining valid information about one's self would seem generally useful.

Finally, at the level of the individual, there are many unanswered questions concerning the development of values. What are the relative roles of educational experiences, family patterns, religious experience and work experience? In short, how do individual manager value patterns develop? The answer to these questions will require long-term longitudinal study of many individual managers and will involve a substantial research investment.

It also is possible to use the PVQ at an organizational or group level. For example, it would be currently topical to compare the personal value systems of male and female managers. Owner-managers of small business establishments have likewise not been studied to any large extent even though they may well provide one of the clearest samples for studying the relationship between value intentionality and actual behavior.

It would also seem useful to analyze the characteristics of organizations which facilitate or hinder the translation of its members' values from the stage of intentionality into behavior. For this purpose, explicit hypotheses would have to be developed and data collected on values as well as actual or simulated behavior from individuals employed in organizations with different characteristics. The possibility of simulating organizational pressures and constraints in laboratory settings also would seem to be a viable approach.

One may employ PVQ data to determine the extent to which conflict within an organization is a function of differing value systems of the participating members or of coalitions of members. People with different value systems may tend to approach various issues from conflicting points of view. Closely linked to these ideas is the question of whether or not there is any optimal value mix within an organization which promotes organizational efficiency and effectiveness. As indicated earlier, our data are not sufficient for this purpose. While we suspect that the relationship between value mix and organizational outcomes would differ among firms of differing size, with differing task structures and facing differing environmental situations, we simply do not know what the relationships are.

A final line of inquiry at the organizational level has to do with the notion of role assumption. To what extent do individuals take on the predominant values of their organization? Do incoming college graduates shift their values to match those of their employing organization? To what extent is one's behavior influenced by the managerial role he assumes as opposed to being influenced by his own personal values? All of these are important questions which could be answered through the use of the PVQ in appropriately designed studies.

At the country or societal level, the PVQ may be utilized to study the personal value systems of various major social or interaction groups. These studies should provide useful input for policy decisions about dealing with such groups. One can also engage in longitudinal studies aimed at analyzing relationships between personal values and economic development, and more specifically, looking at the rate of transformation of value systems at various stages of economic progress. In terms of the theoretical model described earlier, this would imply studying the rate at which nonrelevant values become relevant values and adopted and intended values become operative values.

Managerial value studies would seem relevant to questions about movement toward certain management systems, toward multinational management and toward postindustrial management philosophies and systems. The comparative aspects of our analyses certainly demonstrate these possibilities.

It is our sincere hope that the theory, the methodology, the data and the ideas presented in this book will be worthy of inclusion in a wide range of studies about managers, their values and their behavior.

Appendices

Appendix A

Research Instrument:
Personal Values
Questionnaire

This questionnaire is part of a research study of personal values. The aim of the study is to find out how individuals look at a wide range of topics. These topics are about **people, groups of people, personal goals, organizational goals** and **general ideas.**

You will be asked to judge the degree to which each topic is: (1) important, (2) pleasant, (3) right and (4) successful. In completing this questionnaire, please make your judgments on the basis of what these topics mean to **you** as an individual.

Under no circumstances will your individual responses be made available to anyone except the research workers. The data we are attempting to gather are for use only in our research project on personal values.

In advance we wish to thank you for your participation in this study. It is through cooperation in studies such as this that we all advance our understanding of human behavior.

INSTRUCTIONS

Rate how important a topic is to you by placing an "X" in the appropriate box: the left box signifies high importance; the middle box, average importance; and the right box, low importance.

Then specify which of the three descriptions (successful, pleasant, right) best indicates the meaning of the topic to you; indicate your choice by placing the number "1" on the line next to it. Then indicate which description least indicates the topic's meaning to you by writing the number "3" in the

---

[1] (Minneapolis: University of Minnesota, Industrial Relations Center, 1965). The basic English version of the PVQ is shown. It was used without translation in the study of U.S., Indian and Australian managers and was translated into Japanese and Korean for use in those two countries.

space provided. Finally, write the number "2" next to the remaining description. Complete all topics in this manner and check to see that the three descriptions for each topic have been ranked in the manner instructed.

Examples

As an example, take the topic **Patriotism**. If you felt that it is of average importance, you would make a check mark in the middle box as indicated. If you felt that of the three descriptions (pleasant, right and successful) "right" best indicates what the topic means to you, you would write the number "1" next to "right." If the description "successful" least indicates what the topic means to you, then you would write the number "3" next to "successful," as shown in the sample below. Then you would place the number "2" next to the remaining description, in this case "pleasant."

For some topics you may feel that none of the descriptions apply. For example, you may feel that for the topic **Dishonesty**, neither "pleasant," "right" nor "successful" indicates the meaning to you. If you have this trouble, you may begin by deciding which description least indicates the topic's meaning to you. For example, for the topic **Dishonesty** if you felt that "right" least indicates the topic's meaning to you, you would write the number "3" next to "right," and so on for the remaining descriptions as shown in the sample.

Patriotism		**Dishonesty**	
High Low		High Low	
Importance □ □ □ Importance		Importance □ ⊠ □ Importance	
2 pleasant		2 pleasant	
1 right		3 right	
3 successful		1 successful	

Goals of Business Organizations

High Productivity	**Industry Leadership**	**Employee Welfare**
High Low	High Low	High Low
Imp. □ □ □ Imp.	Imp. □ □ □ Imp.	Imp. □ □ □ Imp.
_____ right	_____ right	_____ right
_____ successful	_____ successful	_____ successful
_____ pleasant	_____ pleasant	_____ pleasant

Organizational Stability	**Profit Maximization**	**Organizational Efficiency**
High Low	High Low	High Low
Imp. □ □ □ Imp.	Imp. □ □ □ Imp.	Imp. □ □ □ Imp.
_____ right	_____ right	_____ right
_____ successful	_____ successful	_____ successful
_____ pleasant	_____ pleasant	_____ pleasant

	Social Welfare		Organizational Growth	
High Imp. □ □ □ Low Imp.			High Imp. □ □ □ Low Imp.	
____ right			____ right	
____ successful			____ successful	
____ pleasant			____ pleasant	

Groups of People

Employees	Customers	My Co-workers
High Imp. □ □ □ Low Imp.	High Imp. □ □ □ Low Imp.	High Imp. □ □ □ Low Imp.
____ right	____ right	____ right
____ successful	____ successful	____ successful
____ pleasant	____ pleasant	____ pleasant
Craftsmen	**My Boss**	**Managers**
High Imp. □ □ □ Low Imp.	High Imp. □ □ □ Low Imp.	High Imp. □ □ □ Low Imp.
____ right	____ right	____ right
____ successful	____ successful	____ successful
____ pleasant	____ pleasant	____ pleasant
Owners	**My Subordinates**	**Laborers**
High Imp. □ □ □ Low Imp.	High Imp. □ □ □ Low Imp.	High Imp. □ □ □ Low Imp.
____ right	____ right	____ right
____ successful	____ successful	____ successful
____ pleasant	____ pleasant	____ pleasant
My Company	**Blue Collar Workers**	**Stockholders**
High Imp. □ □ □ Low Imp.	High Imp. □ □ □ Low Imp.	High Imp. □ □ □ Low Imp.
____ right	____ right	____ right
____ successful	____ successful	____ successful
____ pleasant	____ pleasant	____ pleasant

Technical Employees			Me			Labor Unions		
High Imp. □ □ □ Low Imp.			High Imp. □ □ □ Low Imp.			High Imp. □ □ □ Low Imp.		
____ right ____ successful ____ pleasant			____ right ____ successful ____ pleasant			____ right ____ successful ____ pleasant		
			White Collar Employees					
			High Imp. □ □ □ Low Imp.					
			____ right ____ successful ____ pleasant					

Ideas Associated with People

Ambition	Ability	Obedience
High Imp. □ □ □ Low Imp.	High Imp. □ □ □ Low Imp.	High Imp. □ □ □ Low Imp.
____ right ____ successful ____ pleasant	____ right ____ successful ____ pleasant	____ right ____ successful ____ pleasant
Trust	**Aggressiveness**	**Loyalty**
High Imp. □ □ □ Low Imp.	High Imp. □ □ □ Low Imp.	High Imp. □ □ □ Low Imp.
____ right ____ successful ____ pleasant	____ right ____ successful ____ pleasant	____ right ____ successful ____ pleasant
Prejudice	**Compassion**	**Skill**
High Imp. □ □ □ Low Imp.	High Imp. □ □ □ Low Imp.	High Imp. □ □ □ Low Imp.
____ right ____ successful ____ pleasant	____ right ____ successful ____ pleasant	____ right ____ successful ____ pleasant

Cooperation	Tolerance	Conformity
High Low	High Low	High Low
Imp. ☐ ☐ ☐ Imp.	Imp. ☐ ☐ ☐ Imp.	Imp. ☐ ☐ ☐ Imp.
_____ right	_____ right	_____ right
_____ successful	_____ successful	_____ successful
_____ pleasant	_____ pleasant	_____ pleasant

	Honor	
	High Low	
	Imp. ☐ ☐ ☐ Imp.	
	_____ right	
	_____ successful	
	_____ pleasant	

Personal Goals of Individuals

Leisure	Dignity	Achievement
High Low	High Low	High Low
Imp. ☐ ☐ ☐ Imp.	Imp. ☐ ☐ ☐ Imp.	Imp. ☐ ☐ ☐ Imp.
_____ right	_____ right	_____ right
_____ successful	_____ successful	_____ successful
_____ pleasant	_____ pleasant	_____ pleasant

Autonomy	Money	Individuality
High Low	High Low	High Low
Imp. ☐ ☐ ☐ Imp.	Imp. ☐ ☐ ☐ Imp.	Imp. ☐ ☐ ☐ Imp.
_____ right	_____ right	_____ right
_____ successful	_____ successful	_____ successful
_____ pleasant	_____ pleasant	_____ pleasant

Job Satisfaction	Influence	Security
High Low	High Low	High Low
Imp. ☐ ☐ ☐ Imp.	Imp. ☐ ☐ ☐ Imp.	Imp. ☐ ☐ ☐ Imp.
_____ right	_____ right	_____ right
_____ successful	_____ successful	_____ successful
_____ pleasant	_____ pleasant	_____ pleasant

Power	**Creativity**	**Success**
High Low Imp. □ □ □ Imp. _____ right _____ successful _____ pleasant	High Low Imp. □ □ □ Imp. _____ right _____ successful _____ pleasant	High Low Imp. □ □ □ Imp. _____ right _____ successful _____ pleasant
Prestige		
High Low Imp. □ □ □ Imp. _____ right _____ successful _____ pleasant		

Ideas About General Topics

Authority	**Caution**	**Change**
High Low Imp. □ □ □ Imp. _____ right _____ successful _____ pleasant	High Low Imp. □ □ □ Imp. _____ right _____ successful _____ pleasant	High Low Imp. □ □ □ Imp. _____ right _____ successful _____ pleasant
Competition	**Compromise**	**Conflict**
High Low Imp. □ □ □ Imp. _____ right _____ successful _____ pleasant	High Low Imp. □ □ □ Imp. _____ right _____ successful _____ pleasant	High Low Imp. □ □ □ Imp. _____ right _____ successful _____ pleasant
Conservatism	**Emotions**	**Equality**
High Low Imp. □ □ □ Imp. _____ right _____ successful _____ pleasant	High Low Imp. □ □ □ Imp. _____ right _____ successful _____ pleasant	High Low Imp. □ □ □ Imp. _____ right _____ successful _____ pleasant

Force		
High		Low
Imp. ☐ ☐ ☐ Imp.		
____ right		
____ successful		
____ pleasant		

Government
High   Low
Imp. ☐ ☐ ☐ Imp.
____ right
____ successful
____ pleasant

Liberalism
High   Low
Imp. ☐ ☐ ☐ Imp.
____ right
____ successful
____ pleasant

Property
High   Low
Imp. ☐ ☐ ☐ Imp.
____ right
____ successful
____ pleasant

Rational
High   Low
Imp. ☐ ☐ ☐ Imp.
____ right
____ successful
____ pleasant

Religion
High   Low
Imp. ☐ ☐ ☐ Imp.
____ right
____ successful
____ pleasant

Risk
High   Low
Imp. ☐ ☐ ☐ Imp.
____ right
____ successful
____ pleasant

Personal Information

1. Title of your present position:

_____

2. Present department in company (check one):
   ____ Production
   ____ Operations
   ____ Sales/Distribution
   ____ Engineering
   ____ Finance/Accounting
   ____ Personnel/Industrial Relations
   ____ Public Relations/Advertising
   ____ Research and Development
   ____ General Administration
   ____ Other (please specify) _____

3. Is your position a line or staff job? (check one):
   ____ Line Management
   ____ Staff Management
   ____ Combined Line and Staff

4. How many **levels** of supervision are there in your company (from first level supervisor to president)? (Give number)

_____

5. How many **levels** of supervision are there above your position? (Give number)

_____

6. Time in present position (check one):
   ____ Under 1 year ____ 6-10 years
   ____ 1-3 years   ____ 11-15 years
   ____ 4-5 years   ____ Over 15 years

7. Total time with company (check one):
   ____ 0-1 year   ____ 11-20 years
   ____ 2-3 years ____ 21-30 years
   ____ 4-5 years ____ Over 30 years
   ____ 6-10 years

8. Total time as a manager (check one):
   ____ 0-5 years   ____ 16-20 years
   ____ 6-10 years ____ 21-30 years
   ____ 11-15 years ____ Over 30 years

9. Approximately how many employees (management and nonmanagement) are there in your company? (check one)

_____ 0-49   _____ 5000-9999
_____ 50-99   _____ 10,000-29,999
_____ 100-499   _____ 30,000-99,999
_____ 500-999   _____ 100,000-299,999
_____ 1000-4999 _____ 300,000 or over

10. Type of company you work for (check one):

_____ Agricultural
_____ Mining
_____ Contract Construction
_____ Manufacturing
_____ Transportation and Public Utilities
_____ Wholesale and Retail Trade
_____ Finance, Insurance and Real Estate
_____ Services (e.g., hotels, laundries)
_____ Government
_____ Other (please specify) _____

11. Your age (check one):

_____ 20-29   _____ 45-49
_____ 30-34   _____ 50-54
_____ 35-39   _____ 55-59
_____ 40-44   _____ 60 or over

12. Sex:

_____ Male
_____ Female

13. Formal education (check highest completed):

_____ Some High School
_____ High School Degree
_____ Some College
_____ College Degree
_____ Postgraduate work

14. Major in college (check one):

_____ (Did not attend college)
_____ Humanities
_____ Fine Arts
_____ Engineering
_____ Business Administration
_____ Physical Sciences
_____ Biological Sciences
_____ Social Sciences
_____ Other (please specify) _____

15. Present yearly income from position (check one):

_____ Under $6000
_____ $6000 to $8999
_____ $9000 to $11,999
_____ $12,000 to $14,999
_____ $15,000 to $19,999
_____ $20,000 to $24,999
_____ $25,000 to $34,999
_____ $35,000 to $49,999
_____ $50,000 to $74,999
_____ Over $75,000

16. Choose the **one** of the following statements which best tells how well you like your job. Place a check mark in front of that statement.

_____ 1. I hate it.
_____ 2. I dislike it.
_____ 3. I don't like it.
_____ 4. I am indifferent to it.
_____ 5. I like it.
_____ 6. I am enthusiastic about it.
_____ 7. I love it.

17. Check one of the following to show **how much of the time** you feel satisfied with your job:

_____ 1. All the time.
_____ 2. Most of the time.
_____ 3. A good deal of the time.
_____ 4. About half of the time.
_____ 5. Occasionally.
_____ 6. Seldom.
_____ 7. Never.

18. Check the **one** of the following which best tells how you feel about changing your job:

_____ 1. I would quit this job at once if I could get anything else to do.

_____ 2. I would take almost any other job in which I could earn as much as I am earning now.

_____ 3. I would like to change both my job and my occupation.

_____ 4. I would like to exchange my present job for another job.

_____ 5. I am not eager to change my job, but I would do so if I could get a better job.

_____ 6. I cannot think of any jobs for which I would exchange.

_____ 7. I would not exchange my job for any other.

19. Check **one** of the following to show how you think you compare with other people.

    _____ 1. No one likes his job better than I like mine.

    _____ 2. I like my job much better than most people like theirs.

    _____ 3. I like my job better than most people like theirs.

    _____ 4. I like my job about as well as most people like theirs.

    _____ 5. I dislike my job more than most people dislike theirs.

    _____ 6. I dislike my job much more than most people dislike theirs.

    _____ 7. No one dislikes his job more than I dislike mine.

THANK YOU

Normative Data on Each Value Item

By Concept Data

Percentage of Respondents for Whom a Concept Represents
an Operative, Intended, Adopted or a Weak Value*

	Operative	Intended	Adopted	Weak
1. High Productivity				
International Sample**	68	18	6	8
U.S. Managers	63	18	10	10
Japanese Managers	79	17	2	2
Korean Managers	67	14	3	17
Australian Managers	62	23	8	8
Indian Managers				
Private Sector	62	27	3	8
Public Sector***	67	23	1	9
2. Industry Leadership				
International Sample	40	17	16	27
U.S. Managers	43	14	18	25
Japanese Managers	46	18	16	20
Korean Managers	30	20	17	33
Australian Managers	44	18	11	28
Indian Managers				
Private Sector	38	17	12	33
Public Sector	34	20	19	26

*These figures have been rounded to the closest whole percentage. Totals in each row may not add to 100 percent.

**The international sample consists of 150 managers randomly drawn from each of the five countries—a total sample of 750 managers.

***Data are reported here for the 263 public sector Indian managers although they have not been used in the major analyses.

	Operative	*Intended*	*Adopted*	*Weak*
3. Employee Welfare				
International Sample	34	38	7	21
U.S. Managers	34	32	10	24
Japanese Managers	20	60	3	17
Korean Managers	20	44	6	30
Australian Managers	45	28	9	18
Indian Managers				
Private Sector	44	25	11	20
Public Sector	39	33	9	19
4. Organizational Stability				
International Sample	46	22	12	19
U.S. Managers	41	14	16	28
Japanese Managers	58	25	8	9
Korean Managers	55	16	11	18
Australian Managers	41	19	14	26
Indian Managers				
Private Sector	58	23	9	9
Public Sector	51	24	11	14
5. Profit Maximization				
International Sample	49	15	18	18
U.S. Managers	58	16	14	12
Japanese Managers	61	17	15	8
Korean Managers	45	18	17	20
Australian Managers	38	18	18	26
Indian Managers				
Private Sector	36	17	21	27
Public Sector	30	14	18	37
6. Organizational Efficiency				
International Sample	64	19	8	10
U.S. Managers	65	18	10	7
Japanese Managers	62	19	12	8
Korean Managers	49	13	17	21
Australian Managers	64	25	4	7
Indian Managers				
Private Sector	69	22	5	5
Public Sector	63	29	5	3
7. Social Welfare				
International Sample	16	18	13	53

	Operative	*Intended*	*Adopted*	*Weak*
U.S. Managers	8	7	16	69
Japanese Managers	11	39	8	42
Korean Managers	14	21	7	59
Australian Managers	25	12	18	45
Indian Managers				
Private Sector	18	13	17	52
Public Sector	23	17	13	46
8. Organizational Growth				
International Sample	51	13	17	19
U.S. Managers	47	14	22	18
Japanese Managers	73	15	7	5
Korean Managers	61	14	14	11
Australian Managers	29	11	22	37
Indian Managers				
Private Sector	47	23	12	19
Public Sector	41	24	17	17
9. Employees†				
International Sample	45	30	7	18
U.S. Managers	60	26	5	9
Japanese Managers	44	44	3	10
Korean Managers	38	26	12	24
Australian Managers	57	23	10	10
Indian Managers				
Private Sector	34	18	12	35
Public Sector	35	18	19	28
10. Customers				
International Sample	61	23	6	10
U.S. Managers	71	23	3	4
Japanese Managers	63	24	7	6
Korean Managers	47	20	12	22
Australian Managers	67	24	2	7
Indian Managers				
Private Sector	61	28	5	7
Public Sector	58	28	4	10
11. My Co-workers				
International Sample	30	23	13	33
U.S. Managers	43	25	9	23
Japanese Managers	17	27	12	44
Korean Managers	22	20	18	39

†In case of Indian managers, concept All Employees was used in place of Employees.

	Operative	Intended	Adopted	Weak
Australian Managers	39	21	11	29
Indian Managers				
Private Sector	33	22	14	30
Public Sector	30	17	20	33
12. Craftsmen††				
International Sample	41	15	23	22
U.S. Managers	38	10	27	26
Japanese Managers	38	10	31	21
Korean Managers	42	14	24	20
Australian Managers	42	14	18	26
Indian Managers				
Private Sector	49	17	15	19
Public Sector	49	15	17	20
13. My Boss				
International Sample	38	20	17	26
U.S. Managers	54	22	11	14
Japanese Managers	33	18	18	31
Korean Managers	30	13	20	37
Australian Managers	37	19	16	29
Indian Managers				
Private Sector	41	23	14	23
Public Sector	37	22	15	27
14. Managers				
International Sample	56	17	12	15
U.S. Managers	59	17	12	12
Japanese Managers	63	23	8	6
Korean Managers	57	16	10	17
Australian Managers	51	21	13	14
Indian Managers				
Private Sector	43	20	16	21
Public Sector	39	17	15	28
15. Owners				
International Sample	29	12	20	39
U.S. Managers	39	15	18	28
Japanese Managers	16	9	32	43
Korean Managers	26	11	25	38
Australian Managers	27	13	17	44

††In case of Indian managers, concept Highly Skilled workers was used in place of Craftsman.

	Operative	Intended	Adopted	Weak
Indian Managers				
Private Sector	27	15	17	42
Public Sector	22	14	21	43
16. My Subordinates				
International Sample	50	25	8	17
U.S. Managers	56	25	8	12
Japanese Managers	49	38	5	8
Korean Managers	40	29	11	20
Australian Managers	60	19	8	13
Indian Managers				
Private Sector	40	22	13	25
Public Sector	46	13	14	27
17. Laborers‡				
International Sample	16	6	26	52
U.S. Managers	22	7	27	45
Japanese Managers	5	4	32	60
Korean Managers	9	7	29	56
Australian Managers	24	6	27	43
Indian Managers				
Private Sector	9	8	28	56
Public Sector	9	7	27	58
18. My Company				
International Sample	61	24	6	8
U.S. Managers	69	24	3	5
Japanese Managers	61	27	5	7
Korean Managers	53	20	9	18
Australian Managers	63	26	5	6
Indian Managers				
Private Sector	57	27	6	10
Public Sector	53	23	11	13
19. Blue Collar Workers‡				
International Sample	27	12	26	36
U.S. Managers	28	8	25	38
Japanese Managers	30	20	23	28
Korean Managers	33	18	20	29
Australian Managers	28	7	26	40
Indian Managers				
Private Sector	12	5	34	48
Public Sector	10	7	33	51

‡In case of Indian managers, concepts Unskilled Workers and Semiskilled Workers were used in place of Laborers and Blue Collar Workers respectively.

	Operative	Intended	Adopted	Weak
20. Stockholders				
International Sample	25	15	22	38
U.S. Managers	37	13	20	30
Japanese Managers	24	19	24	33
Korean Managers	21	10	30	40
Australian Managers	24	12	23	42
Indian Managers				
Private Sector	23	13	20	44
Public Sector	14	12	25	49
21. Technical Employees†				
International Sample	57	14	13	15
U.S. Managers	51	14	17	18
Japanese Managers	67	17	10	7
Korean Managers	53	19	14	14
Australian Managers	50	12	16	22
Indian Managers				
Private Sector	56	14	15	15
Public Sector	52	16	15	18
22. Me				
International Sample	41	22	16	21
U.S. Managers	47	21	15	18
Japanese Managers	40	37	8	15
Korean Managers	42	18	15	25
Australian Managers	42	19	16	23
Indian Managers				
Private Sector	32	14	25	30
Public Sector	37	12	21	30
23. Labor Unions				
International Sample	19	15	19	47
U.S. Managers	14	8	31	48
Japanese Managers	17	27	14	42
Korean Managers	15	11	16	59
Australian Managers	26	12	24	38
Indian Managers				
Private Sector	25	14	21	40
Public Sector	29	13	25	33
24. White Collar Employees				
International Sample	28	8	25	39

†In case of Indian managers, concept Technical Staff was used in place of Technical Employees.

	Operative	*Intended*	*Adopted*	*Weak*
U.S. Managers	35	8	25	32
Japanese Managers	23	13	29	36
Korean Managers	22	9	28	41
Australian Managers	29	6	26	39
Indian Managers				
Private Sector	12	6	30	52
Public Sector	11	7	30	52
25. Ambition				
International Sample	43	13	26	19
U.S. Managers	58	17	13	12
Japanese Managers	26	6	42	26
Korean Managers	39	9	34	19
Australian Managers	46	15	19	20
Indian Managers				
Private Sector	49	19	15	17
Public Sector	46	15	19	20
26. Ability				
International Sample	67	19	6	8
U.S. Managers	65	20	7	8
Japanese Managers	74	17	6	4
Korean Managers	68	13	10	10
Australian Managers	64	25	4	7
Indian Managers				
Private Sector	65	21	7	7
Public Sector	62	21	8	9
27. Obedience				
International Sample	21	12	21	46
U.S. Managers	18	11	20	51
Japanese Managers	3	9	24	64
Korean Managers	15	7	27	51
Australian Managers	24	12	22	42
Indian Managers				
Private Sector	44	16	12	28
Public Sector	39	19	16	27
28. Trust				
International Sample	50	43	2	6
U.S. Managers	46	46	1	7
Japanese Managers	34	59	2	5
Korean Managers	52	37	4	7
Australian Managers	60	34	2	5

	Operative	Intended	Adopted	Weak
Indian Managers				
Private Sector	62	25	5	8
Public Sector	55	23	8	15
29. Aggressiveness				
International Sample	34	10	26	30
U.S. Managers	35	8	33	25
Japanese Managers	55	23	14	8
Korean Managers	50	15	19	15
Australian Managers	11	4	36	49
Indian Managers				
Private Sector	16	6	28	51
Public Sector	6	4	31	59
30. Loyalty				
International Sample	40	31	8	21
U.S. Managers	43	37	5	15
Japanese Managers	11	41	7	40
Korean Managers	25	20	17	38
Australian Managers	55	30	6	9
Indian Managers				
Private Sector	60	20	7	13
Public Sector	55	21	10	14
31. Prejudice				
International Sample	4	3	24	69
U.S. Managers	4	6	28	62
Japanese Managers	7	3	21	74
Korean Managers	7	1	18	75
Australian Managers	3	3	27	67
Indian Managers				
Private Sector	3	2	27	68
Public Sector	2	2	26	71
32. Compassion				
International Sample	13	11	17	59
U.S. Managers	16	14	15	56
Japanese Managers	5	12	9	75
Korean Managers	10	10	17	63
Australian Managers	25	15	19	41
Indian Managers				
Private Sector	12	6	29	53
Public Sector	13	5	23	59

	Operative	Intended	Adopted	Weak
33. Skill				
International Sample	58	15	16	11
U.S. Managers	55	16	17	12
Japanese Managers	60	11	18	10
Korean Managers	50	12	25	14
Australian Managers	65	22	7	7
Indian Managers				
Private Sector	61	18	12	9
Public Sector	55	17	13	15
34. Cooperation				
International Sample	55	27	8	10
U.S. Managers	53	27	9	12
Japanese Managers	49	34	8	9
Korean Managers	56	24	7	13
Australian Managers	60	29	5	6
Indian Managers				
Private Sector	57	22	10	11
Public Sector	52	19	13	15
35. Tolerance				
International Sample	23	19	15	43
U.S. Managers	22	17	17	44
Japanese Managers	12	34	9	46
Korean Managers	18	20	20	42
Australian Managers	35	21	11	33
Indian Managers				
Private Sector	28	17	21	33
Public Sector	33	12	19	37
36. Conformity				
International Sample	9	5	23	63
U.S. Managers	2	1	19	79
Japanese Managers	8	8	26	58
Korean Managers	16	8	20	57
Australian Managers	3	2	24	71
Indian Managers				
Private Sector	16	7	27	49
Public Sector	18	9	25	48
37. Honor				
International Sample	32	29	13	26
U.S. Managers	41	46	3	10
Japanese Managers	12	15	25	48

	Operative	Intended	Adopted	Weak
Korean Managers	20	18	24	39
Australian Managers	53	28	5	15
Indian Managers				
Private Sector	43	21	14	22
Public Sector	44	24	11	21
38. Leisure				
International Sample	6	12	15	68
U.S. Managers	3	8	8	81
Japanese Managers	3	11	10	76
Korean Managers	12	16	16	55
Australian Managers	6	13	12	69
Indian Managers				
Private Sector	11	8	27	53
Public Sector	13	6	25	56
39. Dignity				
International Sample	26	22	13	39
U.S. Managers	30	27	11	32
Japanese Managers	9	21	14	56
Korean Managers	16	6	28	50
Australian Managers	28	23	11	38
Indian Managers				
Private Sector	48	22	11	19
Public Sector	49	23	12	17
40. Achievement				
International Sample	62	21	9	8
U.S. Managers	63	21	6	10
Japanese Managers	77	15	5	3
Korean Managers	60	8	19	13
Australian Managers	55	28	6	12
Indian Managers				
Private Sector	64	23	8	5
Public Sector	66	23	4	7
41. Autonomy				
International Sample	30	19	16	35
U.S. Managers	13	8	23	57
Japanese Managers	44	42	5	10
Korean Managers	55	24	11	11
Australian Managers	16	12	20	51
Indian Managers				
Private Sector	24	10	23	44
Public Sector	29	12	22	37

	Operative	*Intended*	*Adopted*	*Weak*
42. Money				
International Sample	23	11	21	45
U.S. Managers	19	10	24	47
Japanese Managers	19	12	24	46
Korean Managers	35	10	26	29
Australian Managers	18	10	17	55
Indian Managers				
Private Sector	22	11	26	41
Public Sector	23	12	20	45
43. Individuality				
International Sample	28	21	15	37
U.S. Managers	33	21	13	33
Japanese Managers	22	28	11	39
Korean Managers	33	20	16	31
Australian Managers	33	20	14	33
Indian Managers				
Private Sector	38	16	18	28
Public Sector	40	18	16	26
44. Job Satisfaction				
International Sample	50	34	6	10
U.S. Managers	51	40	2	8
Japanese Managers	35	45	4	16
Korean Managers	45	20	16	20
Australian Managers	54	42	1	3
Indian Managers				
Private Sector	67	24	4	5
Public Sector	67	27	3	3
45. Influence				
International Sample	18	12	26	44
U.S. Managers	12	6	29	53
Japanese Managers	26	14	26	34
Korean Managers	26	12	26	35
Australian Managers	12	6	28	54
Indian Managers				
Private Sector	19	18	24	48
Public Sector	17	6	25	52
46. Security				
International Sample	29	23	13	35
U.S. Managers	15	15	14	56
Japanese Managers	26	24	12	38

	Operative	Intended	Adopted	Weak
Korean Managers	35	26	21	19
Australian Managers	28	24	12	36
Indian Managers				
Private Sector	40	20	18	22
Public Sector	39	19	17	25
47. Power				
International Sample	10	4	32	54
U.S. Managers	6	2	38	54
Japanese Managers	9	4	29	58
Korean Managers	16	7	29	48
Australian Managers	6	5	29	61
Indian Managers				
Private Sector	20	7	28	46
Public Sector	21	9	29	41
48. Creativity				
International Sample	60	19	9	12
U.S. Managers	53	19	13	15
Japanese Managers	74	19	4	3
Korean Managers	73	15	6	7
Australian Managers	44	25	10	21
Indian Managers				
Private Sector	60	21	9	11
Public Sector	60	21	7	12
49. Success				
International Sample	56	19	10	16
U.S. Managers	52	20	10	18
Japanese Managers	58	14	18	11
Korean Managers	64	11	10	14
Australian Managers	40	28	10	22
Indian Managers				
Private Sector	57	24	7	12
Public Sector	55	23	10	13
50. Prestige				
International Sample	16	13	20	51
U.S. Managers	11	10	21	58
Japanese Managers	13	6	33	48
Korean Managers	10	3	19	68
Australian Managers	10	15	19	57
Indian Managers				
Private Sector	41	19	14	27
Public Sector	32	22	18	28

	Operative	*Intended*	*Adopted*	*Weak*
51. Authority				
International Sample	27	14	23	37
U.S. Managers	29	13	25	32
Japanese Managers	14	19	19	48
Korean Managers	26	10	24	40
Australian Managers	26	12	15	37
Indian Managers				
Private Sector	32	18	23	26
Public Sector	34	10	27	29
52. Caution				
International Sample	24	8	28	40
U.S. Managers	9	4	33	54
Japanese Managers	47	11	27	16
Korean Managers	40	6	29	25
Australian Managers	8	3	35	54
Indian Managers				
Private Sector	26	8	29	38
Public Sector	28	11	26	36
53. Change				
International Sample	24	8	27	41
U.S. Managers	34	13	23	30
Japanese Managers	22	5	33	40
Korean Managers	13	3	30	54
Australian Managers	28	13	26	33
Indian Managers				
Private Sector	19	6	28	47
Public Sector	22	8	23	47
54. Competition				
International Sample	46	13	20	22
U.S. Managers	48	20	16	16
Japanese Managers	47	13	24	17
Korean Managers	37	8	30	25
Australian Managers	38	19	21	23
Indian Managers				
Private Sector	44	18	17	21
Public Sector	46	16	15	22
55. Compromise				
International Sample	17	10	28	45
U.S. Managers	13	6	32	49

	Operative	Intended	Adopted	Weak
Japanese Managers	11	7	37	45
Korean Managers	27	11	22	40
Australian Managers	14	7	31	48
Indian Managers				
Private Sector	16	11	23	50
Public Sector	15	9	23	53
56. Conflict				
International Sample	5	3	31	61
U.S. Managers	6	3	37	54
Japanese Managers	1	3	23	73
Korean Managers	5	0	22	73
Australian Managers	5	5	37	53
Indian Managers				
Private Sector	6	4	32	58
Public Sector	6	5	25	64
57. Conservatism				
International Sample	5	3	26	67
U.S. Managers	9	5	25	61
Japanese Managers	1	2	27	68
Korean Managers	5	1	27	67
Australian Managers	3	3	27	67
Indian Managers				
Private Sector	3	3	25	69
Public Sector	1	2	28	68
58. Emotions				
International Sample	8	8	19	65
U.S. Managers	12	13	20	55
Japanese Managers	4	7	15	75
Korean Managers	9	3	18	70
Australian Managers	14	11	23	53
Indian Managers				
Private Sector	5	3	24	68
Public Sector	3	7	28	62
59. Equality				
International Sample	15	18	16	51
U.S. Managers	16	13	16	55
Japanese Managers	10	28	10	52
Korean Managers	15	26	14	45
Australian Managers	17	6	23	55
Indian Managers				

	Operative	*Intended*	*Adopted*	*Weak*
Private Sector	21	11	23	45
Public Sector	26	14	19	41
60. Force				
International Sample	18	9	30	43
U.S. Managers	6	2	40	52
Japanese Managers	39	17	20	25
Korean Managers	32	14	10	36
Australian Managers	3	2	35	59
Indian Managers				
Private Sector	7	5	32	56
Public Sector	6	2	33	59
61. Government				
International Sample	25	23	18	35
U.S. Managers	25	19	19	36
Japanese Managers	12	29	19	40
Korean Managers	25	32	8	35
Australian Managers	31	23	19	27
Indian Managers				
Private Sector	34	17	19	30
Public Sector	36	17	19	28
62. Liberalism				
International Sample	16	17	17	50
U.S. Managers	6	5	24	66
Japanese Managers	14	34	8	43
Korean Managers	22	34	10	35
Australian Managers	21	13	19	47
Indian Managers				
Private Sector	20	9	23	49
Public Sector	22	13	24	41
63. Property				
International Sample	26	14	24	36
U.S. Managers	31	17	20	32
Japanese Managers	25	12	28	36
Korean Managers	39	15	20	26
Australian Managers	17	15	27	41
Indian Managers				
Private Sector	14	11	30	45
Public Sector	16	10	25	50

	Operative	*Intended*	*Adopted*	*Weak*
64. Rational				
International Sample	43	23	12	22
U.S. Managers	37	23	15	24
Japanese Managers	54	33	6	7
Korean Managers	41	27	10	22
Australian Managers	38	22	15	25
Indian Managers				
Private Sector	40	16	18	25
Public Sector	43	17	16	23
65. Religion				
International Sample	12	12	14	61
U.S. Managers	19	23	12	46
Japanese Managers	3	11	9	77
Korean Managers	9	11	15	64
Australian Managers	12	7	21	60
Indian Managers				
Private Sector	11	8	21	59
Public Sector	10	9	19	62
66. Risk				
International Sample	22	4	38	36
U.S. Managers	28	9	35	27
Japanese Managers	17	7	45	32
Korean Managers	8	2	38	52
Australian Managers	18	8	31	44
Indian Managers				
Private Sector	28	11	29	33
Public Sector	26	10	28	36

Appendix C

Scoring and Data
Analysis Procedures

Each PVQ concept receives a score for each of the scales used to represent a mode of valuation. The primary or power mode of valuation, *importance*, is evaluated on a three point scale—high, average and low, rated from one to three respectively. Secondary modes of valuation are ranked to indicate the meaning a concept has for the respondent. The number of rankings for managers is three. A rank of one indicates that the concept is most associated in meaning with that term and a rank of three indicates that the concept is least associated in meaning with that term.

The scoring of the PVQ is based on the importance rating and the term that is given a rank of one. The terms ranked two and three have been ignored in the scoring thus far, but it is expected that these responses will be studied in further work with the instrument.

The instrument does not yield a total score in the traditional sense, but the probabilities of a respondent making given responses are calculated from his response matrix, the frequency distribution for the total number of concepts which he scored. The first step in scoring the instrument for a respondent is to construct a response matrix of the total number of concepts scored for each individual. Each concept is tallied into the appropriate cell of the matrix according to its importance rating and the secondary mode ranked one. An example of such a matrix for one respondent is shown in Figure C-1.

Thus, this respondent had 38 concepts that were rated as being of "high importance" and were ranked number one on the "right" mode of valuation.

The response matrix is then converted to a matrix with proportions in the cells and margins. These proportions are the proportion of the total number of concepts in that cell. The proportion matrix for the reponse matrix shown in Figure C-1 is presented in Figure C-2.

These proportions are considered as probabilities that a concept will

Figure C-1

	High Importance	Average Importance	Low Importance	Total
Right 1st ranked	38	6	0	44
Successful 1st ranked	3	14	0	17
Pleasant 1st ranked	2	1	2	5
Total	43	21	2	66

be placed in a given cell. Although many different probabilities can be obtained from the matrix, only the following conditional probabilities are generally computed for anlaysis:

P (right)	or P (R)
P (successful)	or P (S)
P (pleasant)	or P (P)
P (high importance)	or P (HI)
P (average and low importance, or not high importance)	or P $(\overline{HI})$
P (right given high importance)	or P (R/HI)
P (successful given high importance)	or P (S/HI)
P (pleasant given high importance)	or P (P/HI)
P (right given not high importance)	or P $(R/\overline{HI})$
P (successful given not high importance)	or P $(S/\overline{HI})$
P (pleasant given not high importance)	or P $(P/\overline{HI})$
P (right and high importance)	or P (R∩HI)
P (successful and high importance)	or P (S∩HI)
P (pleasant and high importance)	or P (P∩HI)

A questionnaire is regarded as incomplete and excluded from analyses if the subject has left blank or has not responded completely to more than 5 percent of the total number of concepts. For example, a PVQ for managers is ineligible if more than three of the 66 are blank or incomplete. Questionnaire data are analyzed in two ways: by examining individuals across concepts (by person analysis); and by examining concepts across individuals (by concept analysis).

Figure C-2

	High Importance	Average Importance	Low Importance	Total
Right 1st ranked	.576	.091	.0000	.667
Successful 1st ranked	.045	.212	.0000	.258
Pleasant 1st ranked	.03	.015	.03	.076
Total	.651	.318	.03	1.0000

BY PERSON ANALYSIS

By person analysis of PVQ data involves looking at responses of an individual across all the concepts in the PVQ. On the basis of his responses, summarized in his response matrix, an individual is classified into one of the following primary value orientations: pragmatic, moralistic, affect or mixed.

The following steps are involved in classifying subjects into one of the above primary orientations:

1. Among the concepts an individual reports as being of high importance, identify the proportion classified as first ranked on each of the scales representing secondary mode of valuation, and select the largest category. More precisely, the following conditional probabilities are computed:

Managers

P (S/HI)
P (R/HI)
P (P/HI)

where terms inside the parentheses are S = successful, R = right, P = pleasant and HI = high importance.

Thus, the first step is to identify the largest conditional probability for an individual.

2. Compare the value of largest conditional probability to its complement. If, for example, the largest conditional probability selected in the first step was P(S/HI), its complement is the probability of responding successful, given a rating of average importance and low importance, or, that is,

P(S/$\overline{\text{HI}}$), where $\overline{\text{HI}}$ refers to average importance plus low importance. If P(S/HI) is greater than its complement P(S/$\overline{\text{HI}}$), then the individual's primary orientation would be pragmatic. If, however, the complement probability is greater, it would imply a mixed value orientation.

In step one, if the two highest conditional probabilities are tied, the difference between each of these conditional probabilities and its complement are calculated. The primary orientation is then represented by the conditional probability having the largest difference between itself and its complement.

Figure C-3 indicates the primary orientation classifications and the decision rules upon which they are based for the PVQ.

3. After the primary orientation has been determined, calculate the value of the joint probability of the cell which constitutes the individual's operative value cell. If this joint probability is less than .15, implying that less than 15 percent of the total concepts in the PVQ are operative values for the individual, his primary orientation is reclassified as mixed.

If the primary orientation is pragmatic, for example, the joint probability of the operative value cell is the probability of responding "successful" and "high importance" or, that is, P(S∩HI). This can be calculated as follows:

$$P(S∩HI) = \frac{\text{Number of concepts rated "successful" and high importance}}{\text{total number of concepts}}$$

Essentially, steps one and two provide the decision rules for determining primary orientation by utilizing the conditional probabilities of the

Figure C-3

Primary Orientation Classification	Decision Rule
Pragmatic	P (S/HI) is the largest P (S/HI) > P (S/$\overline{\text{HI}}$)
Moralistic	P (R/HI) is the largest P (R/HI) > P (R/$\overline{\text{HI}}$)
Affect	P (P/HI) is the largest P (P/HI) > P (P/$\overline{\text{HI}}$)

Note: In all cases, if the complement probability is greater than its principal, it would imply a mixed value orientation.

cells in the "high importance" column. Step three provides a means of determining whether or not this primary orientation should be reclassified by utilizing the joint probability of the operative cell. Several examples will illustrate the application of these decision rules. The first deals with a case in which the primary orientation is identified as moralistic and no reclassification is necessary. In the second example, the primary orientation is determined for a case in which the two largest conditional probabilities are tied. The third, fourth and fifth are examples which illustrate the identification of a mixed primary orientation. In the third and fourth cases this mixed orientation is determined by comparing the value of the largest conditional probability with that of its complement; and in the fith case it is determined by the joint probability of the operative cell.

Example 1: The response matrix in Figure C-4 represents a frequency distribution of the concepts for an individual on the PVQ.

Of the 44 concepts evaluated as being of "high importance," .68 are classified as "right," .30 as "successful," and .02 as "pleasant." Since .68 $[P(R/HI)]$ is the largest of these conditional probabilities, it is compared with its complement, the probability of responding "right" given "average" and "low importance" $[P(R/AI \cap LI)]$, which is 4/22 or .182. The largest conditional probability, .68, is greater than its complement, .182, so this individual is classified as a moralist.

Next the joint probability of the operative cell is examined. The individual in our example is a moralist, therefore, the joint probability of the operative cell is the probability of responding "right" and "high importance," $P(R \cap HI)$, which is 30/66 or .454. Since .454 is greater than the minimal probability value, .15, which is given in the decision rule in step three, the moralistic orientation for this individual is not reclassified.

Figure C-4

	High Importance	Average Importance	Low Importance	Total
Successful 1st ranked	13	15	0	28
Right 1st ranked	30	4	0	34
Pleasant 1st ranked	1	3	0	4
Total	44	22	0	66

Example 2: In a case where the two highest conditional probabilities of the cells in the "high importance" column are tied, the differences between each of these conditional probabilities and its complement are calculated. These differences are then compared and the largest is determined. The primary orientation is then represented by the conditional probability having the largest difference between itself and its complement. Suppose the response matrix for a given individual was as shown in Figure C-5.

      The individual has evaluated 46 concepts as being of "high importance," with .41 classified as "successful," .41 classified as "right" and .17 classified as "pleasant." The complement of the probability of responding "successful" given "high importance" [P(S/HI)] is the probability of responding "successful" given "average" and "low importance" [P(S/AI∩LI)], which is 5/20 or .25. The complement of the probability of responding "right" given "high importance" [P(R/HI)] is the probability of responding "right" given "average" and "low importance" [P(R/AI∩LI)], which is 6/20 or .30. The differences between each conditional probability and its complement are, respectively, .16 and .11. Since the primary orientation is represented by the conditional probability having the largest difference between itself and its complement, this individual is classified as a moralist. The joint probability of the operative cell [P(R∩HI)] is 19/66 or .288; since this value is greater than .15, it is not necessary to reclassify this moralistic orientation.

Example 3: If the value of the largest conditional probability of the cells in the "high importance" column is less than that of its complement, the primary orientation is classified as mixed. The response matrix of concepts in such a case might look like the one presented in Figure C-6.

      The largest conditional probability is 15/32, or .469, which is the probability of responding "right" given "high importance" [P(R/HI)]. Its

Figure C-5

	High Importance	Average Importance	Low Importance	Total
Successful 1st ranked	19	5	0	24
Right 1st ranked	19	6	0	25
Pleasant 1st ranked	8	8	1	17
Total	46	19	1	66

Figure C-6

	High Importance	Average Importance	Low Importance	Total
Successful 1st ranked	12	8	0	20
Right 1st ranked	15	16	2	33
Pleasant 1st ranked	5	7	1	13
Total	32	31	3	66

complement is 18/34, or .529, the probability of responding "right" given "average" and "low importance" $[P(R/AI \cap LI)]$. Since .529 is larger than .469, the primary orientation is classified as mixed.

Example 4: If the value of the largest conditional probability of the cells in the "high importance" column is equal to that of its complement, the primary orientation is classified as mixed. Suppose the response matrix of concepts for a given individual is shown in Figure C-7.

The probability of responding "right" given "high importance" $[P(R/HI)]$ is the largest conditional probability, with a value of 41/41 or 1.00. Its complement is the probability of responding "right" given "average" and "low importance" $[P(R/AI \cap LI)]$, with a value of 25/25, or 1.00. Since 1.00 = 1.00, the primary orientation is classified as mixed.

Example 5: After a primary orientation has been identified given the decision rules regarding conditional probabilities of the cells in the "high importance" column, it may be reclassified as mixed if the value of the joint probability of the operative cell is less than .15, i.e., if less than 15 percent of the total concepts are operative values for an individual. The response matrix of concepts in Figure C-8 provides an example of such a case.

Of the concepts evaluated as being of "high importance" the largest conditional probability is 6/11, or .545. This is the probability of responding "successful" given "high importance" $[P(S/HI)]$. Its complement is the probability of responding "successful" given "average" and "low importance" $[P(S/AI \cap LI)]$, which is 28/55 or .509. Since the value of the largest conditional probability, .545, is greater than that of its complement, .509, this individual is classified as pragmatic. In examining the joint probability of the operative cell, however, we find that the probability of responding "successful" and "high

Figure C-7

	High Importance	Average Importance	Low Importance	Total
Successful 1st ranked	0	0	0	0
Right 1st ranked	41	20	5	66
Pleasant 1st ranked	0	0	0	0
Total	41	20	5	66

Figure C-8

	High Importance	Average Importance	Low Importance	Total
Successful 1st ranked	6	28	0	34
Right 1st ranked	4	20	1	25
Pleasant 1st ranked	1	5	1	7
Total	11	53	2	86

importance" $[P(S \cap HI)]$ is .091, which is less than the minimal .15 established by our decision rule. Therefore, the primary orientation for this individual is reclassified from pragmatic to mixed.

After the primary orientation has been identified for each individual in the sample, the primary orientation for the total group is determined simply by adding up the number of individuals in each primary orientation category.

BY CONCEPT ANALYSIS

By concept analysis of PVQ data involves looking at responses to each concept across all individuals in a sample. In terms of the theoretical model described earlier, a concept may represent an operative, intended, adopted or a weak value for an individual. When this data is aggregated across all individuals in a group, it would show the number of individuals as a proportion of the group for whom the concept is an operative, intended, adopted and a weak value. In this aggregation procedure, individuals with a mixed value orientation are excluded because it is not possible to obtain the needed scores for them.

A concept is classified as an operative value for an individual if it is rated as being of "high importance" and fits his primary orientation. Thus different scores will be used for identifying operative values for individuals with different primary orientations. The following scores are used for this purpose.

Primary Orientation	Score	
Pragmatic	$HI \cap S$	
Moralistic	$HI \cap R$	$HI \cap PO$
Affect	$HI \cap P$	

Intended values are those concepts which are viewed as being of "high" importance" by an individual but do not fit his primary orientation. The following scores are used in identifying these values.

Primary Orientation	Score	
Pragmatic	$HI \cap R$ or P	
Moralistic	$HI \cap S$ or P	$HI \cap \overline{PO}$
Affect	$HI \cap S$ or R	

Adopted values are those concepts which fit the primary orientation of an individual but which he regards as being of only "average" or "low importance." The following scores identify such values for individuals having different primary orientation.

Primary Orientation	Score	
Pragmatic	AI or $LI \cap S$	
Moralistic	AI or $LI \cap R$	$\overline{HI} \cap PO$
Affect	AI or $LI \cap P$	

Weak values are those concepts which are regarded as neither highly important by an individual nor fit his primary orientation. These concepts are identified by the following scores.

Primary Orientation	Score	
Pragmatic	AI or $LI \cap R$ or P	
Moralistic	AI or $LI \cap S$ or P	$\overline{HI} \cap \overline{PO}$
Affect	AI or $LI \cap S$ or R	

Given the above scores for each individual in the group for each of the concepts in the PVQ, the matrix in Figure C-9 is derived by aggregation. As an example, the concept High Productivity is used.

In the matrix, the figures in percent form are shown in parentheses. Thus, it implies that the concept High Productivity is an operative value for 63.4 percent, an adopted value for 9.6 percent, an intended value for 17.5 percent and a weak value for 9.5 percent of U.S. managers. Similar matrixes are prepared for each concept in the PVQ. The by concept data has been utilized mainly for two purposes. The first involves deriving an average value profile for the group being studied. Thus in the above example, High Productivity is classified as an operative value for the U.S. managers as a group. The second way in which these data have been utilized is for analyzing the behavioral relevance of each concept for a group of individuals. For this purpose, the proportion of the group for which a concept is an operative value is utilized, the contention here being that a higher proportion would imply higher behavioral relevance.

Figure C-9. Matrix for Concept High Productivity

	High Importance (HI)	Average-Low Importance ($\overline{\text{HI}}$)	Total
Primary Orientation (PO)	561 (63.4)	85 (9.6)	646 (73.0)
Not Primary Orientation ($\overline{\text{PO}}$)	155 (17.5)	84 (9.5)	239 (27.0)
Total	716 (81.6)	169 (19.1)	885 (100)

Bibliography

Bibliography

Abegglen, J.C. *Management and worker: the Japanese solution.* Tokyo: Sophia University, 1973.

Adams, T.F.M., and Y. Kobayashi. *The world of Japanese business.* Tokyo: Kodansha International Ltd., 1969.

Adorno, T.W. et al. *The authoritarian personality.* New York: Harpers, 1950.

Alexander, R.A., G.V. Barrett, B.M. Bass and E.C. Ryterband. Empathy, projection and negation in seven countries. In L.E. Abt and B.F. Riess, eds. *Clinical psychology in industrial organization*, pp. 29-49. New York: Gruene and Stratton, 1971.

Allport, G.W. and P.E. Vernon. *A study of values.* Boston: Houghton Mifflin, 1931.

Allport, G.W., P.E. Vernon and G. Lindzey. *Study of values: a scale for measuring the dominant interests in personality*, 3rd ed. Boston: Houghton Mifflin, 1960.

Altschul, C.R. Managerial attitudes: an exploratory cross cultural construct validation. Unpublished master's thesis, Iowa State University, 1970.

Ballon, R.J. *The Japanese employee.* Tokyo: Sophia University, 1969.

Bass, B.M. and L.D. Eldridge. *Transnational differences in the accelerated manager's willingness to budget for ecology.* Management Research Center, University of Rochester, Technical Report No. 50, November 1972.

Barnard, C.I. *Function of the executive.* Cambridge, Massachusetts: Harvard University Press, 1938.

Bray, D.W. and D.L. Grant. The assessment center in the measurement of potential for business management. *Psychological Monographs* 80 (1966).

Bray, D.W., D.L. Grant and W. Katkovsky. Contributions of projective techniques to the assessment of management potential. *Journal of Applied Psychology* 5 (1967):226-32.

Brislin, R.W., W.J. Lonner and R.M. Thorndike. *Cross-cultural research methods.* New York: John Wiley and Sons, 1973.

Brogden, H.E. The primary personal values measures by the Allport-Vernon test, 'A Study of Values.' *Psychological Monographs* 66, no. 16 (1952).

Brunson, R.W. A behavioral case study of a mini-conglomerate. Unpublished doctoral dissertation, Michigan State University, 1970.

Campbell, J.P., M.D. Dunnette, E.E. Lawler and K.E. Weick. *Managerial behavior, performance and effectiveness.* New York: McGraw-Hill Book Co., 1970.

Chowdhry, K. *Change-in-Organizations.* Bombay, India: Lalvani Publishing House, 1970.

Chowdhry, K. Social cultural factors and managerial behavior in organizations. *Social and Cultural Background of Labor-Management Relations in Asian Countries.* Proceedings of the 1971 Asian Regional Conference on Industrial Relations, The Japan Institute of Labour, Tokyo, Japan, 1971.

Clark, A.W. and S. McCabe. Leadership beliefs of Australian managers. *Journal of Applied Psychology* 54 (1970):1-6.

Dicken, C.F. and J.D. Black. Predictive validity of psychometics evaluations of supervisors. *Journal of Applied Psychology* 49 (1965):34-47.

Duffy, E.A. and W.J.E. Crissy. Evaluative attitudes as related to vocational interest and academic achievement. *Journal of Abnormal and Social Psychology* 35 (1940):226-45.

Dwivedi, R.S. The relative importance of personality traits among Indian managers. *Indian Management* 9 (1970):30-35.

England, G.W. Organizational goals and expected behavior of American managers. *Academy of Management Journal* 10, no. 2 (June 1967):107-17.

England, G.W. Personal value systems of American managers. *Academy of Management Journal* 10, no. 1 (1968):53-68.

England, G.W. and Kyong-Dong Kim. Personal value systems of Korean managers. *The Journal of Asiatic Research* 11, no. 2 (June 1968).

England, G.W. and T.J. Keaveny. The relationship of managerial values and administrative behavior. *Manpower and Applied Psychology* 3, nos. 1 and 2 (Winter 1969):63-75.

England, G.W. and R. Koike. Personal value systems of Japanese managers. *Journal of Cross-Cultural Psychology* 1, no. 1 (Spring 1970):21-40.

England, G.W., N.C. Agarwal and R.E. Trerise. Union leaders and managers: a comparison of value systems. *Industrial Relations* 10, no. 2 (May 1971).

England, G.W. and R. Lee. Organizational goals and expected behavior among American, Japanese and Korean managers—a comparative study. *Academy of Management Journal* 14, no. 4 (1971):425-38.

England, G.W. and R. Lee. Organizational size as an influence on perceived organizational goals: a comparative study among American, Japanese, and Korean managers. *Organizational Behavior and Human Performance* 9, 1 (1973):48-58.

England, G.W. and M.L. Weber. Managerial success: A study of value and demographic correlates. Technical Report Number AD747953 prepared under contract number ONR N00014-68-A-0141-003, August 1972.

England, G.W. and R. Lee. The relationship between managerial values and managerial success in the United States, Japan, India and Australia. *Journal of Applied Psychology* 59, 4 (1974):411-19.

England, G.W. and N.C. Agarwal. *Personal value systems and behavior of Australian managers.* Perth, Australia: University of Western Australia, in press.

England, G.W., O.P. Dhingra and N.C. Agarwal. Personal value systems and behavior of Indian managers. *Organization and Administrative Science*, in press.

Eysenck, H.J. *The psychology of politics.* New York: Frederick A. Praeger, Inc., 1954.

Fallding, H. A proposal for the empirical study of values. *American Sociological Review* (1966):223-33.

Ghiselli, E.E. *The validity of occupational aptitude tests.* New York: Wiley, 1966.

Guth, W. and R. Tagiuri. Personal values and corporate strategies. *Harvard Business Review* (September-October 1965):123-32.

Haire, M., E. Ghiselli and L. Porter. *Managerial thinking: an international study.* New York: John Wiley, 1966.

Harmon, H.H. *Modern factor analysis.* Chicago: University of Chicago Press, 1967.

Hinrichs, J.R. Comparison of "real life" assessments of management potential with situational exercises, paper and pencil ability tests, and personal inventories. *Journal of Applied Psychology* 53 (1967):425-32.

Hofstede, G.H. Experiences with G.W. England's personal values questionnaire in an international business school. Working Paper 74-3. Brussels: European Institute for Advanced Studies in Management, February 1974.

Jacob, P.E. *Values and the active community.* New York: The Free Press, 1971.

Jacques, E. *The changing culture of a factory.* London: Tavistock Publications, 1961.

Jain, S.C. *The Indian manager.* Bombay, India: Somaiya Publications, 1971 (especially pp. 168-84).

Jurgensen, C.D. Report to participants on adjective wordsort. Unpublished report, Minneapolis Gas Company, 1966.

Kashefi-Zihajh, M. An empirical investigation of the relationship between value systems and organizational effectiveness. Unpublished doctoral dissertation, Michigan State University, 1970.

Katzell, R.A. Cross-validation of item analyses. *Educational and Psychological Measurement* 11 (1951):16-22.

Kluckhohn, C. Values and value-orientation in the theory of action. In T. Parsons and E. Shils, eds., *Towards a general theory of action*, pp. 388-433. Cambridge: Harvard University Press, 1951.

Kluckhohn, F.R. and F. Strodtbeck. *Variations in value orientations.* New York: Row Peterson and Co., 1961.

Laurent, H. The validation of aids for the identification of managerial potential. Standard Oil of New Jersey (1962).

Laurent, H. Cross-cultural cross validation of empirically validated tests. *Journal of Applied Psychology* 54 (1970):417-23.

Likert, R. *The human organization.* New York: McGraw-Hill Book Co., 1967.

Lurie, W.A. A study of Spranger's value types by the method of factor analysis. *Journal of Social Psychology* 8 (1937):17-37.

Lusk, E.J. and B.L. Oliver. *The impact of organizational interactions on the American manager's personal value system.* Philadelphia: The Wharton School, University of Pennsylvania, 1972.

Mahoney, T.A., T.H. Jerdee and A.N. Nash. *The identification of management potential.* Dubuque, Iowa: Wm. C. Brown Co., 1961.

Mahoney, T.A. Criteria of organizational effectiveness. Mimeographed report, Industrial Relations Center, University of Minnesota, 1966.

McClelland, C.D., J.W. Atkinson, R.A. Clark and E.L. Lowell. *The achievement motive.* New York: Appleton-Century-Crofts, 1953.

McClelland, C.D. *The achieving society.* Princeton, New Jersey: Van Nostrand, 1961.

McLaughlin, G. Values in behavioral science. *Journal of Religion and Health* (1965).

McMurry, R. Conflicts in human values. *Harvard Business Review* (May-June 1963), pp. 130-45.

Mead, R.D. An experimental study of leadership in India. *Journal of Social Psychology* 72 (1967):35-43.

Mead, R.D. and J.D. Whittaker. A cross-cultural study of authoritarianism. *Journal of Social Psychology* 72 (1967):3-7.

Mitchell, V.F. and L.W. Porter. Comparative managerial role perceptions in military and business hierarchies. *Journal of Applied Psychology* 51 (1967):449-52.

Mobley, W.H. and E.A. Locke. The relationship of value importance to satisfaction. *Organizational Behavior and Human Performance* (1970), pp. 463-83.

Morris, C. *Varieties of human values.* Chicago: University of Chicago Press, 1956.

Moddie, A.D. The making of an Indian executive. *Indian Management* 9, 8 (August 1970):43-49.

Neghandi, A.R. and S.B. Prasad. *Comparative management.* New York: Appleton-Century-Crofts, 1971.

Osgood, E.C., G.J. Suci and P.H. Tannenbaum. *The measurement of meaning.* Urbana: University of Illinois Press, 1957.

Pareek, U. A motivational paradigm of development. *Journal of Social Issues* (1968), pp. 119-20.

Pathak, V.K. Organizational setting, value attitudes and modernization of management. *Indian Journal of Industrial Relations* 6, 1 (1970):41-68.

Patton, A. Deterioration in top executive pay. *Harvard Business Review* 32 (1965):106-18.

Porter, L. and E. Ghiselli. The self-perceptions of top and middle management personnel. *Personnel Psychology* 10 (1957):397-406.

Rokeach, M. *Beliefs, attitudes and values.* San Francisco: Jossey Bass, Inc., 1968.

Rowland, V.K. *Managerial performance standards.* New York: American Management Association, 1960.

Rummell, R.J. *Applied factor analysis.* Evanston: Northwestern University Press, 1970.

Shartle, C. A theoretical framework for the study of behavior in organizations. In A. Halpin, ed. *Administrative theory in education.* Chicago: University of Chicago, Midwest Administration Center, 1958.

Shartle, D., G. Brumbeck and J. Rizzo. An approach to dimension of values. *Journal of Psychology* 57 (1964):101-11.

Sikula, A.F. Values and value systems: Importance and relationship to managerial and organizational behavior. *The Journal of Psychology* 78 (1971):277-86.

Simon, H. On the concept of organization goal. *Administrative Science Quarterly* 10 (1964):1-22.

Singer, H.A. A crises in values. Unpublished manuscript, June 1973.

Smith, B.E. and J.M. Thomas. Cross cultural attitudes among managers: a case study. *Sloan Management Review* (Spring 1972), pp. 35-51.

Spranger, E. *Types of men.* Translated by P.J.W. Pigors of 5th German edition of *Lebensformen.* Halle: Niemeyer, 1928.

Strong, E.K., Jr. Vocational interest 18 years after college. Minneapolis: University of Minnesota Press, 1955.

Subramaniam, V. The managerial class of India. New Delhi: All India Management Association, 1971.

Tagiuri, R. Value orientations and the relationship of managers and scientists. *Administrative Science Quarterly* (1965), pp. 39-51.

Thiagarajan, K.M. A cross-cultural study of the relationship between personal values and managerial behavior. Unpublished doctoral dissertation, University of Pittsburgh, 1968.

Triandis, H.C. Cultural influences upon cognitive processes. In Berkowitz, L., ed., *Advances in social psychology*, vol. 1, pp. 1-48. New York: Academic Press, 1964.

Udy, S.H. *Organizations of work.* New Haven: HRAF Press, 1959.

Weber, M. *The Protestant ethic and the spirit of capitalism.* Translated by Talcott Parsons. London: Allen and Unwin, 1950.

White, J.K. and R.A. Ruh. Effects of personal values on the relationship between participation and job attitudes. *Administrative Science Quarterly* 18 (1973):506-14.

Whitehill, A.M. and S. Takezawa. *The other worker.* Honolulu: East-West Center Press, 1968.

Williams, R.E. A description of some executive abilities by means of the critical incident techniques. Unpublished doctoral dissertation, Columbia University, 1956.

Wollowich, H.G. and W.J. McNamara. Relationship of the components of an assessment center to management success. *Journal of Applied Psychology* 53 (1969):348-52.

Yoshino, M. *Japan's managerial system.* Cambridge, Massachusetts: The MIT Press, 1968.

Zurcher, L.A. Particularism and organizational position: a cross-cultural analysis. *Journal of Applied Psychology* 52 (1968):139-44.

Index

Abegglen, J.C., 35
Adams, T. and Kobayashi, Y., 98
achievement, 5; and India profile, 95; and success scores, 70
affect: and lack of success/satisfaction, 125; and manager orientation, 19; national range, 52; operative values, 107; U.S. managers, 85
aggression, 5; behavior relevance, 28; value in Japan/Korea, 34
Allport, G., et al., 3, 88
ambition, 5; behavior relevance, 28
Australia: concept expectations, 57; homogeneity, 42; humanistic orientation, 34; intended values, 109; manager behavior, 6; moralism, 125; moralistic management, 20; pragmatism, 79; profile, 89-91; profit and growth emphasis, 30; sample selection, 13; success scores, 66; weight of personal goals, 32

Ballon, R., 35
Barnard, Chester, 94
behavior: adopted value, 110; interpretation and value system, 22; and PVQ, 53; situation dependent, 102; success measurement, 62; and value system, 1
Bray, D. and Grant, D., 71; and Katkovsky, W., 70
Brunson, R., 69

Campbell, J., et al., 71
Chowdhry, K., 31
compassion, 5
competition, 5

concepts: adopted value, 110; Australian profile, 89-91; cluster analysis, 71; Confucianism in Japan, 70; development of and PVQ scale, 3; expectations, values, and behavior, 57; of groups of people and PVQ, 33; and High Productivity, 23; and India profile, 91-96; and intentionality, 124; national range and variation, 36

decisionmaking: cross-national, 83; influence of personal values, 58; and Japanese values, 98; and PVQ, 6; and value system, 11, 123
Dicken, C. and Black, J., 71

efficiency, 25
egalitarianism, 91; among Korean managers, 102; and weak values, 111
employee: welfare of, 5; welfare in Japan, 30; welfare and U.S. managers, 121

Ghiselli, E., 59
goals: achievement oriented, 108; and India value system, 92; individual profile, 116; internalization, 97; internalization and impact, 30; as motivation, 25; and national differences, 31

Haire, M., et al., 28, 32, 95
Harmon, H., 42
homogeneity: and cross-country differences, 79; differences, 123; lack of between countries, 51; and pragmatism, 105; in U.S., 88; and value systems, 40

About the Author

George W. England earned his Ph.D. from the University of Minnesota and is currently Professor of Psychology and Industrial Relations at the University of Minnesota. He is the author of *Problems in Vocational Counseling* (Wm C. Brown Co., 1960), *The Development and Use of Weighted Application Blanks* (Wm C. Brown Co., 1961), *The Manager and The Man* (Kent State University Press, 1974). He has published approximately seventy scholarly articles in such journals as *Academy of Management Journal, Personnel Psychology, Journal of Cross-Cultural Psychology, Organization Behavior and Human Performance, Organization and Administration Sciences, Industrial Relations* and *Personnel Administration.*